PALM
DECODER

PALM
DECODER

Read your palm
and foretell your future

TRE McCAMLEY

Quantum
Books

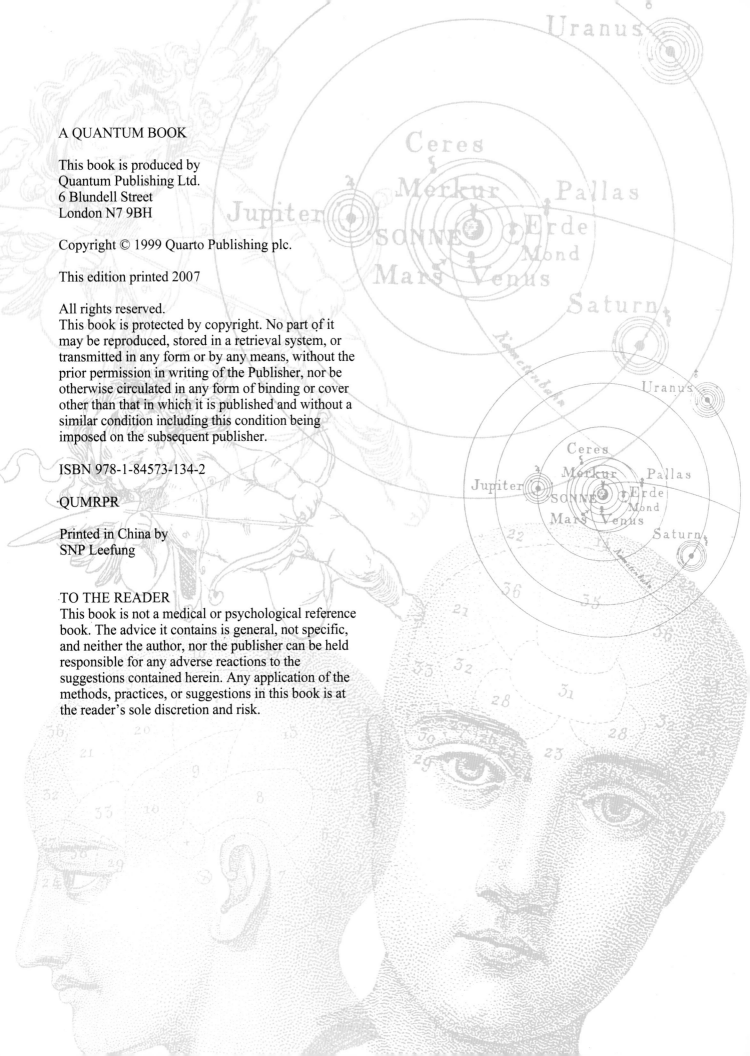

A QUANTUM BOOK

This book is produced by
Quantum Publishing Ltd.
6 Blundell Street
London N7 9BH

ISBN 978-1-84573-134-2

QUMRPR

Printed in China by
SNP Leefung

TO THE READER
This book is not a medical or psychological reference
book. The advice it contains is general, not specific,
and neither the author, nor the publisher can be held
responsible for any adverse reactions to the
suggestions contained herein. Any application of the
methods, practices, or suggestions in this book is at
the reader's sole discretion and risk.

CONTENTS

INTRODUCTION 6

PALMISTRY: GENERAL PRINCIPLES 8

SETTING THE SCENE 10

MAPPING THE HAND 12

INSTANT IDENTIFIER 18

THE MOUNTS 30

LIFE LINE 42

HEART LINE 60

HEAD LINE 74

SIMIAN LINE 90

FATE LINE 96

SUCCESS LINE 112

ATTACHMENT LINE 122

GIRDLE OF VENUS 130

STRESS LINES 136

SPECIAL MARKINGS OF THE PALM 140

INDEX 144

INTRODUCTION

Every person has a unique life story, and our hands contain the coded information that tells us what makes each of us different. A new palm, whether craggy or smooth, is the palmist's equivalent of a new book, with its own fascinating story to tell.

Palmistry, also known as chiromancy and hand analysis, is the most personal of the self-discovery systems. It helps us to understand our personalities, potential, limitations, talents, strengths, and abilities. Also, the lines on your hands will change over time, revealing new information, so you will be able to consult this book time and time again.

This method of palm reading is completely non-psychic and can be learned and put into practice by anybody. By comparing features of your palm with the photographs of hands in this book, you will be able to build up a palm profile and monitor its changing patterns.

This is a working book. Referring to it regularly will help you to map the changes in your life. Use this book when you have decisions to make, but try to keep track of it—the day you lend it to a friend may be the very day you need it!

THE BENEFITS OF PALMISTRY

In palmistry, the hand is the mirror of the soul. A huge amount of information is displayed in your hands, and palmistry is the key that unlocks and translates the secrets of who you really are, revealing your past, present, and potential for the future.

Palmistry is all about you and what is most important to you—whether it be money, love, your career, and so on. You can be your own personal therapist: with every palm reading session, you will begin to feel that you understand yourself a little better. As an individual, you will learn to minimize your weaknesses and take advantage of your strengths.

MAKING DECISIONS

Should I change my job? Am I in love with the right person?

Non-psychic palmistry is a consistent method for making decisions. Learn the technique and you can carry it with you, in your mind, wherever you go.

→ Palmistry helps you to find your professional path.

→ Palmistry answers questions by unlocking secrets and reviving forgotten memories.

→ Palmistry helps you toward personal growth.

→ Palmistry encourages self-understanding, and generates new thoughts and ideas.

→ Palmistry helps you to recognize mindtraps and to overcome unproductive thinking.

→ Palmistry reveals opportunities.

→ Palmistry helps to sharpen and clear the mind.

Reading palms, either your own or others', is always exciting. People will naturally open up to you when you express an interest in deciphering their palms. You may find that you start to notice palms everywhere—whether you are in the bank discussing a loan with the manager, or at work, asking for a pay raise from your boss.

PALMISTRY:
GENERAL PRINCIPLES

The hands are home to a disproportionately high number of the body's nerve ending receptors. This makes your palms the best place to chart physical, emotional, and medical history, intellect, potential achievement, and changes in your life's path. The basic principles of the art of palm reading are described over the next few pages.

WHICH PALMISTRY?

There are three basic types of palmistry: Oriental palmistry, Asian palmistry, and Western palmistry. Oriental and Asian palmistry rely heavily on skin patterns, fingertip patterns, symbols with the appearance of animals, and the lines that run around the wrist called the rascettes or bracelets of life. These types of palmistry focus much more than Western palmistry on the extended family and on everyday decisions.

The main focus of Western palmistry is you.

WHICH HAND DO YOU READ?

The DOMINANT HAND is the hand you write with and reveals the conscious self—your outward personality, what you have made and will make of your life, and your medical history.

The PASSIVE HAND is your other hand and reveals the unconscious self—your inner personality, your life's potential, and your family medical history.

By comparing the readings of each hand you will have an idea of how your actual life matches or differs from your inner potential.

Remember, the future is not cast in stone. Humans are powerful creatures that can and do change the paths they follow. Lines can break, breaks can heal, and lines can become weaker or stronger. Some lines will change within a few weeks, others will change fundamentally over a few years.

For the best and most enjoyable palm readings, you must be completely at ease. Try to choose a time of day when you are less likely to be disturbed. Create a relaxed and stress-free atmosphere with natural light or soft lighting at night. Shine a desk light across the palm to enhance detail. Soft, pleasant music and lightly scented candles will help create the right mood. A magnifiying glass is useful to see details both in the hand you are reading and the palms in this book. A soft cushion to rest your hand on with the palm facing upward will help the hand to adopt its natural position.

MINDSET

Before you start your reading, relax, breathe deeply, and clear your mind. You do not need to be psychic. It is a matter of simply interpreting the lines and translating them as you would from one language to another. If you keep an open mind, you will achieve much, much more. Your hands are the book of your life.

STARTING A READING

On an acetate sheet and using a water-based fiber-tip pen, draw around your dominant hand, palm down. Turn your hand and the acetate over and mark the main lines as shown below. (You can reposition and mark more of your lines later.)

Using the Instant Identifier section on pages 18–29, match the shape of each line to one of the many examples. To find out the meanings, refer to the indicated pages that show the closest match for each line on your hand. Result: your very own palm reading!

Once you have marked all your lines on the acetate, photocopy it, and write down the date, then wipe the acetate clean and start again with the passive hand. Where the lines differ, interpret the lines on the passive hand as features of the inner person or latent self.

If you experience any difficulty drawing and interpreting several lines together, simply start again with the outline of the hand and just work on one line at a time.

For an in-depth reading, follow the same procedure but take care to draw breaks, islands, and other markings as accurately as possible. Details of each of the various specific markings are all found in this book. Check each line carefully and you will build up a full and accurate palm reading.

MAPPING THE HAND

THE MAIN LINES

The lines on your hand are indicators of major influences and movements in your life. Identify each line on your palm by checking its position and path. Remember that not every line will show up on different palms.

GIRDLE OF VENUS
pages 130–135

HEART LINE
pages 60–73

HEAD LINE
pages 74–89

LIFE LINE
pages 42–59

STRESS LINES
pages 136–139

ATTACHMENT
LINES
pages 122–129

APOLLO LINE
(SUCCESS LINE)
pages 112–121

FATE LINE
(CAREER LINE)
pages 96–111

ASSESSING LINES

The quality of each line and the patterns that are formed around it are the signs that will help you to do your interpretation and make your reading.

One useful working theory for assessing lines is to imagine each line as a steadily flowing river. A clearly defined, even line is a river and a life running smoothly. This may help you to remember the subtle changes in meaning that each line variation brings. Are you in for a bumpy ride? Is the river blocked and you need to go another way?

UNEVEN LINE

Uneven lines are deep in some places, showing strength and intensity, and shallow in others, showing spent energy and weakness.

SPLIT LINE

A line that splits, with branches running close to the main line then stopping, shows energy wasted on unfinished projects. A wide, long branch leading to a mount shows attraction to the qualities of that mount.

ISLANDS

An island is formed by a line splitting from a main line then rejoining it. Islands show energy weakened by flowing in two directions, then strength of purpose renewed as the lines combine.

BREAKS

Breaks stop the natural flow in some way. A small break or overlapping broken ends will have a minimal effect.

SQUARES

A square is a protective barrier that forms particularly around a break or weakness in a line, like a reinforcement on a riverbank. This indicates that someone is caring for you in times of difficulty.

CHAINED LINE

A chained line shows a path that is labored, strained, or obstructed in some way. Think of that river with its force divided. Chaining on the heart line shows sentimentality, and on the head line shows that you are prone to headaches.

SISTER LINES

A line appearing alongside and parallel to weakness on another line is called a sister line, and protects and strengthens the main line.

PALM SIGNS

Signs or symbols may be found on the palm in a number of places. The interpretations of the symbols that follow have been proven right time and time again.

TRIANGLES

An isolated triangle on the palm shows great mental brilliance. A triangle on the mount at the base of the index finger highlights lofty ambition.

STARS

Stars illuminate. When a star appears in any area—formed by three lines crossing at a single point—it signifies brighter, better, and generally more fortunate prospects.

SQUARES

A notable square found on the mount at the base of the index finger, is the teacher's square. This indicates a person whose talent lies in teaching and coaching.

PHALANXES OF THE THUMB

The top phalanx of the thumb, which contains the nail, represents willpower. The lower phalanx, below the joint, represents logic. Normally, they are about the same length. A shorter top phalanx shows a lack of willpower.

A long, lower phalanx denotes a very logical person. Lines cutting across the lower phalanx are called intuition rings—the more rings there are, the greater the intuition. These lines often signify the seemingly contradictory condition of a very logical, yet highly intuitive individual.

FINGERPRINT PATTERNS

Every person's fingerprint patterns, as we know from their use in police department records, are unique. They can give us further clues to a person's nature and strengths.

ULNAR LOOP

The ulnar loop points toward the thumb and is the most common fingerprint pattern. It shows someone who is adaptable and versatile in changing circumstances.

RADIAL LOOP

The radial loop points away from the thumb and shows a versatile, adaptable, and also rather extroverted personality.

COMPOSITE LOOP

The composite loop looks like the letter S, with two loops lying in opposite directions. This shows an often indecisive individual, who sees both sides of a problem and is pulled in both directions.

WHORL (ISLAND)

A whorl looks like the ripples made by a stone dropped into a pond, and indicates people who "island" themselves by concentrating solely on a particular task. This usually means a leader or a non-conformist who holds strong personal views, and often denotes success, particularly when seen on the index and/or ring finger.

PEACOCK'S EYE

This is a whorl enclosed in a loop. The characteristics are the same as for the whorl but the loop adds luck, protection, and penetrating perception.

ARCH

A small arch denotes the need to provide protection and security, and shows a person who is driven to a sense of responsibility, but often feels it as a burden. The arch, though infrequent, usually appears on more than one finger, exaggerating its effect.

PALMAR RIDGES

Fingerprint patterns as they appear on the palm are known as palmar ridges. As a general rule, your body is in good balance when the skin ridges on your palm are clear and the skin is springy when pressed with a finger. Examination of the palmar ridges can reveal a variety of imbalances and health conditions. Although its usage is likely to become much more widespread over the next few years, it is not within the scope of this book to go into this fascinating area, called dermataglyphics, in any detail.

CHILDREN LINES

These are the lines that cross the attachment lines at right angles. Recent palmistry research has shown no conclusive correlation between children lines and the

number of children you are likely to have, despite the predictions and claims made by palmists over the years. Perhaps today, the children lines reflect potential rather than actual children in a world where successful contraception, greater emphasis on career, and increased negative stress affect people's decisions or capacity to have children.

As a result, children lines signify your level of empathy with children.

INSTANT IDENTIFIER

The Instant Identifier section shows a reduced reproduction of all the palms featured in this book and is designed to help you find a quick match for your palm. Trace your palm on the acetate sheet, look through the reduced palms to find the closest match, then turn to the page number listed.

FREQUENTLY ASKED QUESTIONS

Q: My life line has a high start and a forked end. In which section do I look?

A: Look in both sections. Any line can comprise more than one set of features. Simply combine the interpretations given for each feature to make a fuller reading. The examples in this book are designed to show each feature at its clearest, but there are many variations.

Q: Why are there so many lines on my hand?

A: Probably because you have a full hand. First, compare your hand to the hands in the stress lines section: finding the dominant lines through a maze of stress lines is a common problem for palmists today. The best way to tackle your hand is to carefully examine each line one at a time.

Q: What happens to the lines when I make a major life change?

A: Lines on your hand change over the course of your life. If you make a major life change that is not shown on your palm map, the lines will change accordingly within a few months. It is worth making a photocopy of your hand with some current notes, then monitoring changes as they happen.

Q: What do I do if the palm that matches mine is on the wrong hand?

A: No problem. Reverse the acetate so that a left hand becomes a right hand, or a right hand becomes a left hand. The only thing you need to remember is whether it is the dominant or passive hand.

Q: My lines are not exactly the same as on the closest matching palm. What does this mean?

A: Lines vary from person to person. The palms in this book have been chosen to illustrate the most important features. The additional information for each hand may or may not apply to you, so browse through other pages to spot features that match your own.

Q: I have just a few lines. Does this mean my life is fairly uninteresting?

A: There is no such thing as a boring palm. Each palm has a unique, fascinating story, which the palmist is privileged to glimpse. Having just a few lines often makes readings more straightforward.

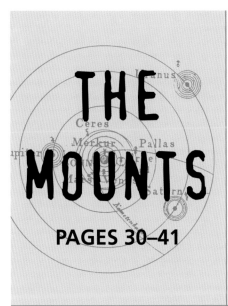

THE MOUNTS

PAGES 30–41

MOUNT OF JUPITER
● WELL-DEVELOPED

PAGE 32

MOUNT OF SATURN
● WELL-DEVELOPED

PAGE 33

MOUNT OF APOLLO
● WELL-DEVELOPED

PAGE 34

MOUNT OF MERCURY
● WELL-DEVELOPED

PAGE 35

MOUNT OF VENUS
● WELL-DEVELOPED

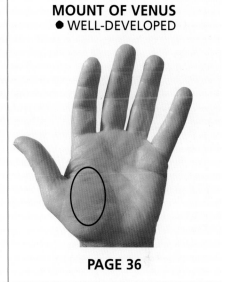

PAGE 36

MOUNT OF LUNA
● WELL-DEVELOPED

PAGE 37

MOUNT OF NEPTUNE
● WELL-DEVELOPED

PAGE 38

MOUNT OF MARS NEGATIVE
● WELL-DEVELOPED

PAGE 39

MOUNT OF MARS POSITIVE
- WELL-DEVELOPED

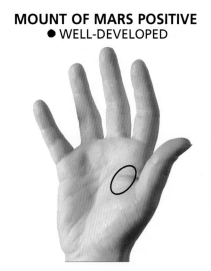

PAGE 40

MOUNT OF VENUS/
MOUNT OF NEPTUNE
- WELL-DEVELOPED

PAGE 41

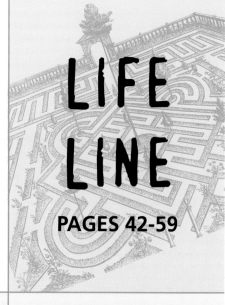

LIFE LINE

PAGES 42-59

LIFE LINE
- RUNS WIDE AROUND THUMB
- WELL-DEVELOPED VENUS
  MOUNT

PAGE 47

LIFE LINE
- APPEARS TO BE SHORT
- APPEARS TO BE BROKEN

PAGE 48

LIFE LINE
- APPEARS TO BE SHORT
- APPEARS TO BE BROKEN

PAGE 49

LIFE LINE
- FULL • FORKED END

PAGE 53

LIFE LINE
- ENDS TUCKED UNDER
  BALL OF THUMB

PAGE 54

LIFE LINE
- ENDS SWEEPING AWAY
  FROM THUMB

PAGE 55

LIFE LINE
- RUNS CLOSE TO THUMB
- NARROW VENUS MOUNT

PAGE 44

LIFE LINE
- RUNS CLOSE TO THUMB
- NARROW VENUS MOUNT

PAGE 45

LIFE LINE
- RUNS WIDE AROUND THUMB
- WELL-DEVELOPED VENUS MOUNT

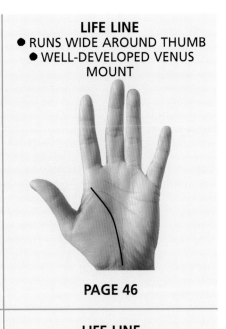

PAGE 46

LIFE LINE
- SHORT
- HAS A BREAK IN IT

PAGE 50

LIFE LINE
- DOUBLE
- FULL OR PARTIAL

PAGE 51

LIFE LINE
- FULL
- FORKED END

PAGE 52

LIFE LINE
- STARTS HIGH

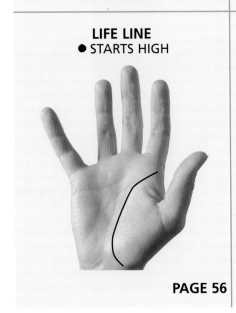

PAGE 56

LIFE LINE
- STARTS LOW
- CLOSER TO THUMB

PAGE 57

LIFE LINE
- PASSIVE
- DIFFERENCES FROM DOMINANT

PAGE 58

LIFE LINE
- DOMINANT
- DOUBLE
- FULL OR PARTIAL

PAGE 59

HEART LINE

PAGES 60–73

HEART LINE
- ENDS UNDER THE INDEX FINGER
- ENDS ON THE JUPITER MOUNT

PAGE 65

HEART LINE
- ENDS BETWEEN THE INDEX AND MIDDLE FINGER

PAGE 66

HEART LINE
- ENDS BETWEEN INDEX AND MIDDLE FINGER

PAGE 67

HEART LINE
- DOUBLE
- PARALLEL ANYWHERE

PAGE 71

HEART LINE
- PASSIVE
- DIFFERENCES FROM DOMINANT

PAGE 72

HEART LINE
- DOMINANT
- ENDS ON INDEX FINGER

PAGE 73

HEART LINE
- SHORT ● STRAIGHT
- ENDS UNDER MIDDLE FINGER

PAGE 62

HEART LINE
- SHORT ● STRAIGHT
- ENDS UNDER MIDDLE FINGER

PAGE 63

HEART LINE
- LONG ● STRAIGHT
- ENDS UNDER INDEX FINGER

PAGE 64

HEART LINE
- FORKED END ● TRIDENT END

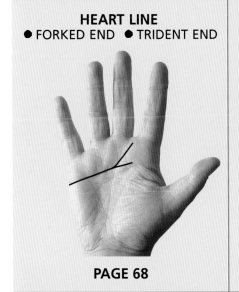

PAGE 68

HEART LINE
- STRONG ● CLEAR

PAGE 69

HEART LINE
- MANY BRANCHES

PAGE 70

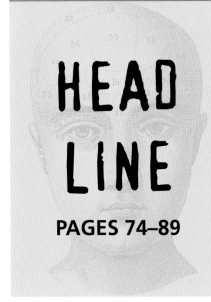

HEAD LINE

PAGES 74–89

HEAD LINE
- SHORT ● STRAIGHT
- ENDS UNDER MIDDLE FINGER

PAGE 76

HEAD LINE
- LONG ● STRAIGHT ● ENDS
UNDER RING OR MIDDLE FINGER

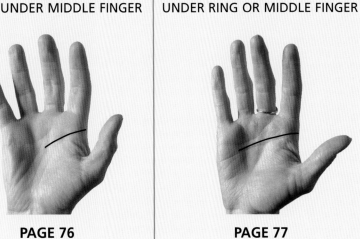

PAGE 77

HEAD LINE
- LONG • CURVES DOWNWARD

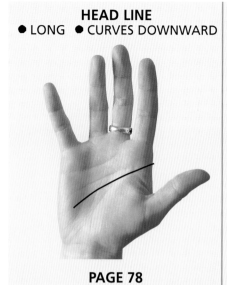

PAGE 78

HEAD LINE
- LONG • DIPS SHARPLY

PAGE 79

HEAD LINE
- STARTS CONNECTED TO LIFE LINE

PAGE 80

HEAD LINE
- ENDS IN AN UPWARD FORK

PAGE 84

HEAD LINE
- ENDS IN A DOWNWARD FORK

PAGE 85

HEAD LINE
- TRIDENT END

PAGE 86

SIMIAN LINE

PAGES 90–95

SIMIAN LINE
- STRAIGHT ACROSS PALM
- NO HEAD LINE
- NO HEART LINE

PAGE 92

HEAD LINE
● STARTS COMPLETELY SEPARATE FROM THE LIFE LINE

PAGE 81

HEAD LINE
● STARTS HIGH ● CLOSER TO INDEX FINGER THAN THUMB

PAGE 82

HEAD LINE
● STARTS LOW ● CLOSER TO THUMB THAN INDEX FINGER

PAGE 83

HEAD LINE
● DOUBLE ● PART OR FULL

PAGE 87

HEAD LINE
● LONG ● DIPS SHARPLY

PAGE 88

HEAD LINE
● DOMINANT ● DIFFERENCES FROM PASSIVE

PAGE 89

SIMIAN LINE
● WITH HEART LINE
● WITH HEAD LINE

PAGE 93

SIMIAN LINE
● STRAIGHT ACROSS PALM
● NO HEART OR HEAD LINES
● PASSIVE ● SAME ON BOTH HANDS

PAGE 94

SIMIAN LINE
● STRAIGHT ACROSS PALM
● NO HEART OR HEAD LINES
● DOMINANT

PAGE 95

FATE LINE

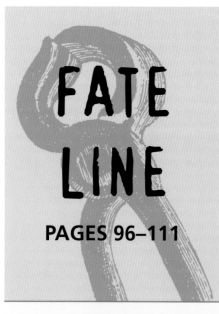

PAGES 96–111

FATE LINE
● STRAIGHT ● CLEARLY DEFINED

PAGE 98

FATE LINE
● APPEARS TO STOP AND START

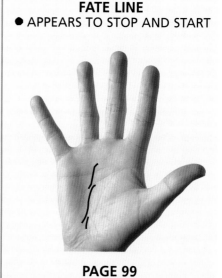

PAGE 99

FATE LINE
● ENDS HIGH ON PALM
● STOPS AT BASE OF FINGERS

PAGE 103

FATE LINE
● ENDS TOWARD INDEX FINGER

PAGE 104

FATE LINE
● WITH A LINE STRIKING IT
● UPWARD JOINING BRANCH

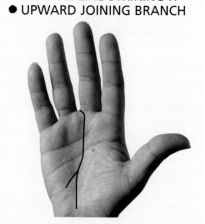

PAGE 105

FATE LINE
● DOUBLED FOR ANY
OF ITS LENGTH

PAGE 109

FATE LINE
● STARTS FROM LIFE LINE
● PASSIVE

PAGE 110

FATE LINE
● DOMINANT
● DIFFERENCES FROM PASSIVE

PAGE 111

FATE LINE
● STARTS HIGH ON THE PALM

PAGE 100

FATE LINE
● STARTS ON LUNA MOUNT

PAGE 101

FATE LINE
● STOPS FAR SHORT OF THE BASE OF THE FINGERS

PAGE 102

FATE LINE
● STARTS ON VENUS MOUNT

PAGE 106

FATE LINE
● MULTIPLE ENDS

PAGE 107

FATE LINE
● DOUBLED FOR ANY OF ITS LENGTH

PAGE 108

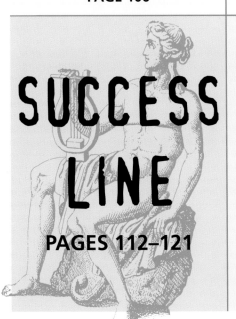

SUCCESS LINE
PAGES 112–121

SUCCESS LINE
● SHORT
● STARTS IN TOP HALF OF PALM

PAGE 114

SUCCESS LINE
● FAINT

PAGE 115

SUCCESS LINE
- STARTS WITH A STAR

PAGE 116

SUCCESS LINE
- AS THREE LINES • UPWARD FROM THE HEART LINE

PAGE 117

SUCCESS LINE
- MULTIPLE
- REFLECTS FATE LINE

PAGE 118

ATTACHMENT LINE

PAGES 122–129

ATTACHMENT LINE
- FORKED END

PAGE 124

ATTACHMENT LINE
- HAS A BREAK • REJOINS

PAGE 125

ATTACHMENT LINE
- STRAIGHT • CLEAR

PAGE 129

GIRDLE OF VENUS

PAGES 130–135

GIRDLE OF VENUS
- FULL SEMI-CIRCLE • AROUND BASE OF MIDDLE FINGERS

PAGE 132

SUCCESS LINE
- MULTIPLE
- REFLECTS FATE LINE

PAGE 119

SUCCESS LINE
- DOMINANT - DIFFERENCES FROM PASSIVE

PAGE 120

SUCCESS LINE
- LONG

PAGE 121

ATTACHMENT LINE
- DIPS
- RUNS DOWN PALM

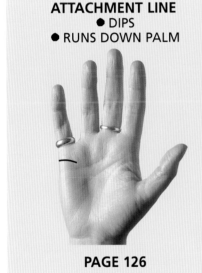

PAGE 126

ATTACHMENT LINE
- DIPS
- RUNS DOWN PALM

PAGE 127

ATTACHMENT LINE
- RISES SHARPLY

PAGE 128

GIRDLE OF VENUS
- CONNECTED TO ATTACHMENT LINE

PAGE 133

GIRDLE OF VENUS
- PARTIAL - SHORT BETWEEN MIDDLE AND RING FINGERS

PAGE 134

GIRDLE OF VENUS
- PARTIAL - SHORT BETWEEN INDEX AND MIDDLE FINGERS

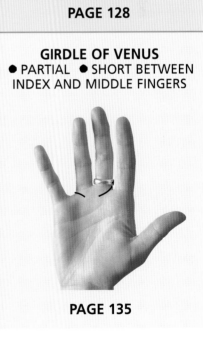

PAGE 135

WHAT DRIVES YOU?
THE MOUNTS

Mounts represent the driving forces in your life. The most developed mounts on your palm, the dominant mounts, are the ones that most affect you. Feeling your mounts to determine their size is called mount manipulation and is a wonderful and soothing activity, whether you have it done for you or you do it for others.

Initially, the best way to find your dominant mounts is to use a light, exploratory touch to locate the padded areas of your palm without actually looking at it. When you have a rough idea of the areas which feel more swollen or raised, gently cup your palm and look at it. You will be able to see the mounts stand out. Do not worry if the mounts at the base of the fingers seem offset, this is completely normal.

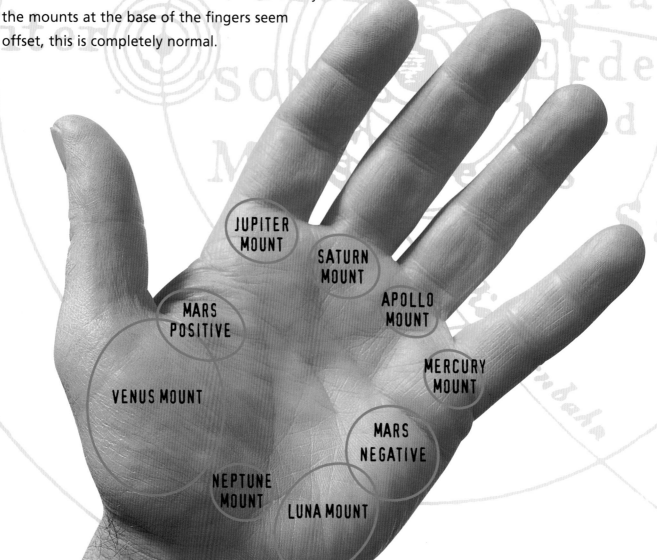

JUPITER MOUNT

SATURN MOUNT

APOLLO MOUNT

MARS POSITIVE

MERCURY MOUNT

VENUS MOUNT

MARS NEGATIVE

NEPTUNE MOUNT

LUNA MOUNT

LOCATION

THE MAJOR MOUNTS:

JUPITER MOUNT	Located at the base of the index finger.
SATURN MOUNT	Located at the base of the middle finger.
APOLLO MOUNT	Located at the base of the ring finger.
MERCURY MOUNT	Located at the base of the little finger.
VENUS MOUNT	Located at the base of the thumb.
LUNA MOUNT	Located at the opposite edge of the palm from the Venus mount.

THE MINOR MOUNTS:

NEPTUNE MOUNT	Located between the Venus mount and the Luna mount, and adjacent to the wrist.
MARS NEGATIVE	Located at the side of palm opposite to thumb, between the Luna mount and the Mercury mount.
MARS POSITIVE	Located at the side of palm between the index finger and thumb.

FIVE COMMONLY ASKED QUESTIONS:

→ Why do I feel the need to work hard and play hard?

→ Am I a natural-born leader?

→ Why is communication most important to me?

→ I often sit daydreaming and constructing novels in my mind. What does it mean?

→ Why do I need people around me to "come alive"?

MOUNT OF JUPITER

• WELL-DEVELOPED

You are wise and have great business acumen and leadership qualities. A full mount of Jupiter is often associated with island fingerprint patterns. The development of the mount slightly toward the middle finger shows high morals and a well-developed sense of justice and ambition. An overdeveloped mount indicates that these personal characteristics have become exaggerated: generosity has become extravagance, and enterprise has become pompous self-importance or arrogance.

MYSTIC CROSS:
In the quadrangle formed between the heart and head lines, your mystic cross highlights an interest in the occult or paranormal or the rediscovery of a psychic gift. You have great intuition or a sixth sense, manifested in business deals, often of a speculative nature.

Complementary readings

RAJAH LOOP:
The loop pattern between your index and middle fingers was historically thought to denote a blood connection with royalty. This is a unique sign.

LUNA MOUNT:
A developed lower Luna mount, appearing almost to overhang your wrist, is another sign of someone particularly gifted and perceptive.

MOUNT OF JUPITER

MOUNT OF SATURN

● WELL-DEVELOPED

Stability, seriousness, and a love of tradition in your life are emphasized. A high mount can mean an overserious predisposition and stern outlook, but the gently rounded mount here is more likely to show your interest in study and research, or perhaps reveals an unnecessarily pessimistic view of marriage prospects. Despite the stern implications of a developed mount of Saturn, the opposite picture—a warm personality—appears in your hand.

Complementary readings

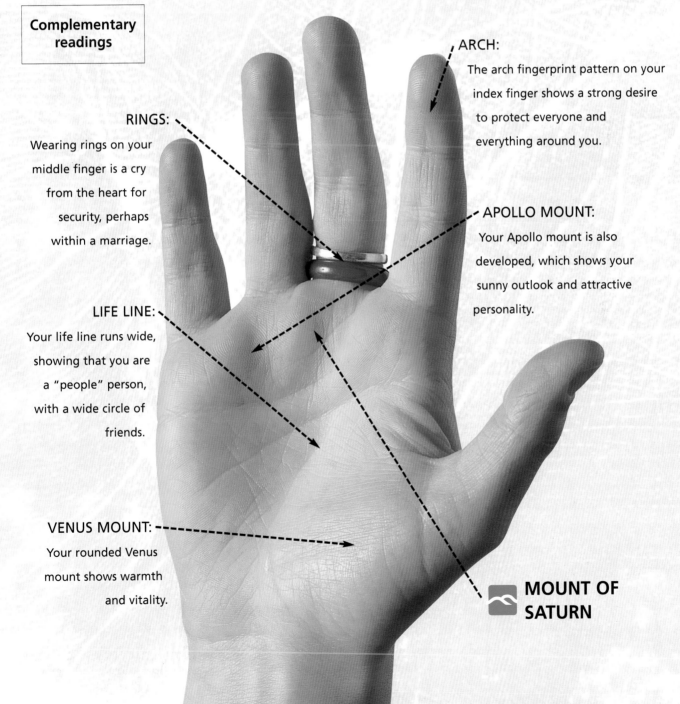

ARCH:
The arch fingerprint pattern on your index finger shows a strong desire to protect everyone and everything around you.

RINGS:
Wearing rings on your middle finger is a cry from the heart for security, perhaps within a marriage.

APOLLO MOUNT:
Your Apollo mount is also developed, which shows your sunny outlook and attractive personality.

LIFE LINE:
Your life line runs wide, showing that you are a "people" person, with a wide circle of friends.

VENUS MOUNT:
Your rounded Venus mount shows warmth and vitality.

MOUNT OF SATURN

MOUNT OF APOLLO

● WELL-DEVELOPED

Associated with money, fun, enjoyment, recreation, and success, your developed Apollo mount shows you to have a definite talent for television work. You are unfailingly optimistic, and there is a strong chance that fortune will shine on you and everything you do.

Complementary readings

FATE LINE:

Although there are a number of twists and turns throughout your career, it is significant that both a success line and a business line spring from your fate line. A little work effort will go a long way toward success.

MOUNT OF APOLLO

LIFE LINE:

In your mid to late teens, there is a break in your life line with a connection to a stronger line running wide around the ball of your thumb. An emigration to a new life with more comfort and a wider range of prospects is a strong possibility.

VIA LASCIVIA:

The horizontal, low line running from the edge of the palm away from the thumb is known as a via lascivia. Historically misunderstood as a sign of a debauched lifestyle, today this is known as an allergies line, indicating a sensitivity to stimulants.

MOUNT OF MERCURY
● WELL-DEVELOPED

You are a great communicator with a keen working intuition. A developed Mercury mount also reflects good business acumen, quickness, and perhaps surprisingly, sexuality. Your mount has a refined, even texture, which reflects your approach to communication.

Complementary readings

MOUNT OF MERCURY

SOLOMON RING:

The ring around the base of your index finger is a mark of wisdom and leadership. Because both verbal and nonverbal communication are central to good leadership, your ability to convey information unambiguously is vital. A Solomon ring on only the dominant hand shows a sometimes reluctant leader, but one who is the best person for the job. A Solomon ring on only the passive hand shows an inner, prevailing need to take control.

FATE LINE:

Your fate line has two starts, one from your life line, showing a possible link to a family profession, and one from the creative Luna mount. In your twenties, the two jobs, or parts of the job, come together but not for long. You seem more at ease with variety and settle in later years to successful self-employment.

MOUNT OF VENUS

● WELL-DEVELOPED

You are a "people" person, full of vitality, with a warm and loving nature. A large Venus mount shows a real zest for life, and can highlight virility. You need to be loved. The depth and size of the mount, with its firm and springy appearance, corresponds to inner resilience and reserves of energy. Larger than life, you have a capacity to work hard and play hard.

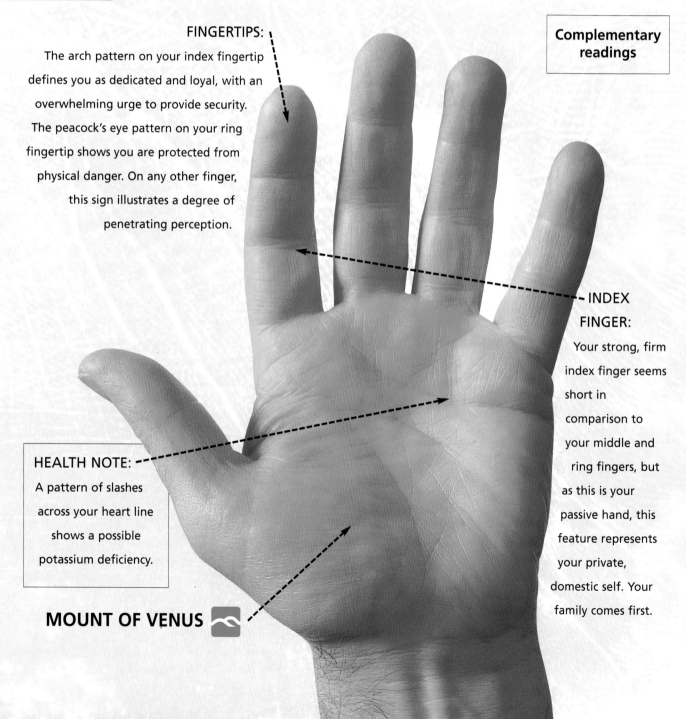

FINGERTIPS:
The arch pattern on your index fingertip defines you as dedicated and loyal, with an overwhelming urge to provide security. The peacock's eye pattern on your ring fingertip shows you are protected from physical danger. On any other finger, this sign illustrates a degree of penetrating perception.

Complementary readings

INDEX FINGER:
Your strong, firm index finger seems short in comparison to your middle and ring fingers, but as this is your passive hand, this feature represents your private, domestic self. Your family comes first.

HEALTH NOTE:
A pattern of slashes across your heart line shows a possible potassium deficiency.

MOUNT OF VENUS

MOUNT OF LUNA

● WELL-DEVELOPED

You are creative and probably have a love of nature. Sensitive to moods, you are drawn to water. The low, bulging edge of your palm next to the Luna mount shows a potential interest in mysticism. A bulge so low that it almost overhangs the wrist shows a psychic talent and an interest in the paranormal. This is also the mount of the subconscious—if it is soft to the touch, you may be a dreamer who sees great things but never achieves them. However, in your case, the thumb, index finger, and Venus mount are all strong which shows you are an achiever and not just a dreamer.

1.5

Complementary readings

APOLLO MOUNT:
A developed Apollo mount shows you have a sunny outlook and an attractive personality, but that you also seek the achievement of material prosperity and success.

ISLANDS:
Island patterns on all your fingertips show you are sure to obtain success in anything you set out to achieve. Not a team player but a team leader, you are the one who sets the example.

MOUNT OF LUNA

CURVED LOOP:
The curved loop coming into your Luna mount area shows an affinity with water.

1.6

MOUNT OF NEPTUNE

• WELL-DEVELOPED

You have a charismatic, magnetic personality. Quick, perceptive, and charming, you are very likely a performer. You may utilize intuition as an aid to communication, and you are likely to have an interest in the spiritual and in mysticism. Neptune and Apollo mounts are both developed, showing that you work hard but play hard too.

Complementary readings

HEAD LINE:
Your independent head line starts on the Jupiter mount, running straight across the palm to the opposite edge. Your focus on business and leadership is reinforced by a strong and intensely directed work ethic.

INDEX FINGER:
Your index finger is very strong and thickly rooted, showing ambition with a strong business sense.

APOLLO MOUNT:
With a full Apollo mount, you have a great sense of fun.

HEAD LINE:
A depression, or blocking point, halfway along your head line reflects problems when you try to focus your thoughts. Given your business strengths, you find this immensely frustrating.

MOUNT OF NEPTUNE

MOUNT OF MARS NEGATIVE

● WELL-DEVELOPED

Also known as the mount of upper Mars, this mount is at the edge of the palm opposite the thumb, occupying the middle section. A high palm edge, like a thick rim, shows you are a principled person who works well under pressure. Passive resistance and grim determination characterize your remarkable endurance.

Complementary readings

MIDDLE FINGER:
A ring on the middle finger shows a yearning for security, which may be provided by a stable and lasting partnership.

LITTLE FINGER:
The second joint of your little finger is enlarged on the inside only, showing you to be sensual with an erotic frame of mind, qualities illustrated again by the third phalanx being the largest.

FINGER SPACING:
The wide space between your index finger and your middle finger, and between your ring finger and little finger, reflects independence of thought and action.

THUMB:
The long first phalanx of your thumb reveals strong willpower. Your thumbtip appears to have a flexible joint, but only the tip bends, indicating versatility and capability.

MOUNT OF MARS NEGATIVE

1.8

MOUNT OF MARS POSITIVE

● WELL-DEVELOPED

Also known as lower Mars, this mount is about physical courage and a fighting spirit. You are courageous and adventurous. A well-developed mount on a hand of a lower type could mean a very argumentative and confrontational person, even an aggressive one, but here it points to your love of a challenge. There is a line of courage crossing this mount, showing you to be a person who stands by whoever or whatever you believe in.

Complementary readings

HEAD LINE:
The independent head line start shows your independence of spirit. You are a risk taker.

MOUNT OF MARS POSITIVE

MARS NEGATIVE:
Mars negative is also well-developed, showing moral courage, ethics, and integrity.

LUNA MOUNT:
You have an investigative interest in the paranormal, shown by a developed lower Luna mount.

MOUNT OF VENUS, MOUNT OF NEPTUNE

• WELL-DEVELOPED

A "people" person, you know how to draw attention and admiration to yourself. You do your best work when dealing with the general public. Your developed Venus mount shows a warm, loving nature, vitality, and a zest for life. You need to be loved. With your developed Neptune mount, you have a charismatic and magnetic personality. Quick, perceptive, and charming, you may be a performer, using intuition to aid communication.

1.9

Complementary readings

SIMIAN LINE: Your fused head and heart lines, defined as a simian line, display the intensity and focus you apply to anything you undertake. You are a person who always goes for it, and gets it.

MOUNT OF NEPTUNE

MOUNT OF VENUS

WILL YOU HAVE A LONG AND SUCCESSFUL LIFE?

LIFE LINE

The life line represents your general personality, life possibilities, the state of your health, and difficulties and successes as you navigate the maze of life. It may be short, straight, curved, or forked. Short life lines must never be assumed to denote a short life—on the contrary, the characteristics of a short line can mean a brand new life. Faintness or islands on the life line can indicate medical problems, trips to hospital, or other health-related issues. This section describes and illustrates many palms with variations to the life line.

FIVE COMMONLY ASKED QUESTIONS:

→ Will I emigrate?

→ My "short" life line worries me; does it mean a short life?

→ I have had so many traumas in my life, will this current calm period continue?

→ How will my health be in the future?

→ Will I pass my exams?

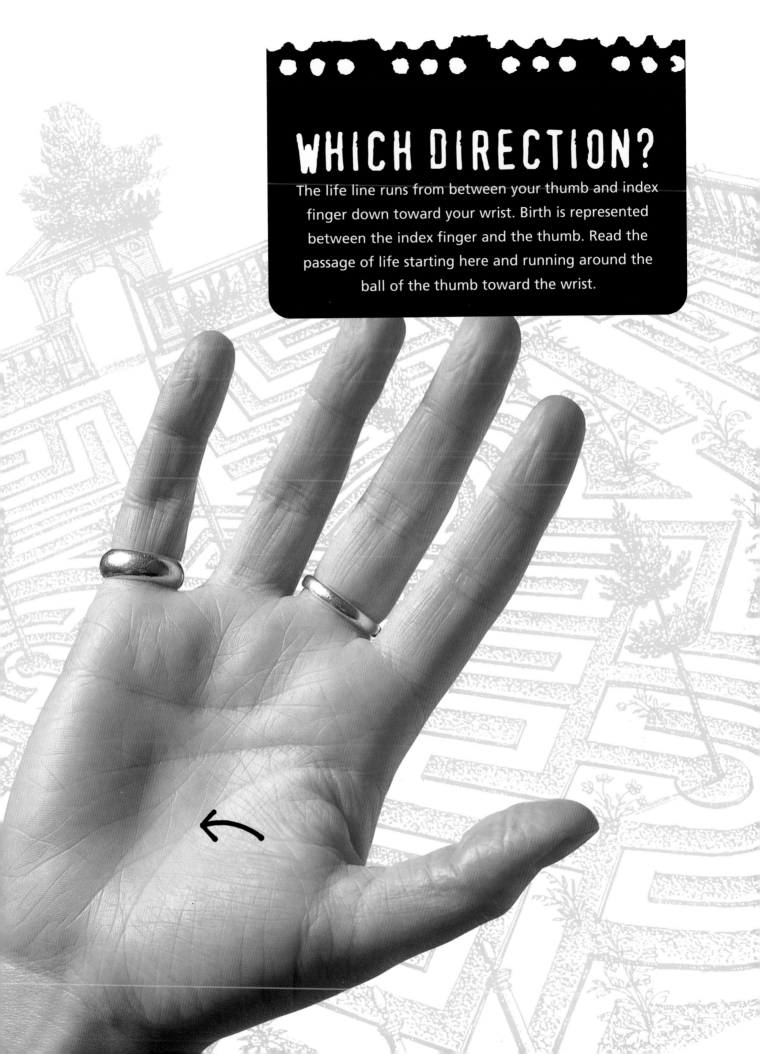

WHICH DIRECTION?

The life line runs from between your thumb and index finger down toward your wrist. Birth is represented between the index finger and the thumb. Read the passage of life starting here and running around the ball of the thumb toward the wrist.

◢◣ LIFE LINE

- **LINE RUNS CLOSE TO THUMB**
- **NARROW VENUS MOUNT**

You are shrewd and businesslike. Knowing how to keep a secret, you also keep issues and problems very much to yourself. With your life line starting high, you are a person who is single-minded and ambitious.

TOP PHALANX:
The top phalanx of your thumb is fairly long, showing strong willpower.

MOUNT OF JUPITER:
Your mount of Jupiter is well-developed, revealing ambition in the field of business.

FATE LINE:
The fate line appears to stop at the center of the palm, but it is actually a double fate line with a second part taking over from the first. Your job or career does not stop, but a second, more compulsive career becomes much more fulfilling.

Complementary readings

FRUSTRATION LINE:
The lines crossing the tip at right angles are frustration lines, suggesting that challenges to your willpower are likely to happen frequently.

THE THUMB:
The thumb, naturally held close, means that you tend to keep ideas, feelings, fears, and emotions in check, even when your partner wants to share them with you.

◢◣ **LIFE LINE**

LIFE LINE

- ● LINE RUNS CLOSE TO THUMB
- ● NARROW VENUS MOUNT

You are shrewd and businesslike. Inclined to be introverted, you know how to keep a secret, but also keep issues, problems, and feelings to yourself. Your life line has a number of lines crossing it at right angles. Signifying dramatic incidents, these trauma lines seem to cease around the age of thirty. Around the late forties, you have a line going to the fate line and back to the life line, which may mean a major relocation or emigration, followed by a return home.

Complementary readings

LIFE LINE

FINGERS:
Some of your fingers show an island pattern, a sign of concentration and focus that signifies success.

THE STAR:
The star on Apollo is a clear sign of fame and fortune.

TEACHER'S SQUARE:
The teacher's square visible on the mount of Jupiter shows your ability to convey information effectively. It does not necessarily mean that your career is in teaching.

FATE LINE:
Your fate line starts with a fork, which usually indicates vocational study as well as a job. The fork is the merging of the two, with the stronger line showing it is a good career decision.

HEAD LINE:
Your head line ends firmly in the mount of Luna, a creative and artistic area.

2.2

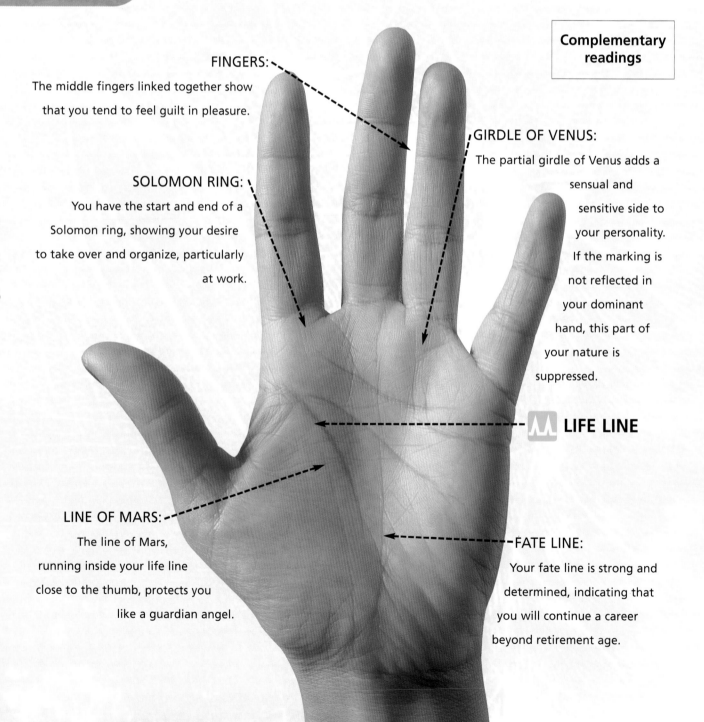 LIFE LINE

- RUNS WIDE AROUND THE THUMB
- WELL-DEVELOPED VENUS MOUNT

You are a "people" person with a wide circle of friends and interests. Your life line shows an emigration around middle age. As you are right-handed and this is your left hand, your parents have moved from their country of birth. Two trauma lines cross your life line at right angles, signifying two significant events between the ages of twenty and thirty, which may be bad or good. Your life line continues straight, deep, and clear, reflecting a clear path in life with few serious health considerations.

Complementary readings

FINGERS:
The middle fingers linked together show that you tend to feel guilt in pleasure.

SOLOMON RING:
You have the start and end of a Solomon ring, showing your desire to take over and organize, particularly at work.

GIRDLE OF VENUS:
The partial girdle of Venus adds a sensual and sensitive side to your personality. If the marking is not reflected in your dominant hand, this part of your nature is suppressed.

LIFE LINE

LINE OF MARS:
The line of Mars, running inside your life line close to the thumb, protects you like a guardian angel.

FATE LINE:
Your fate line is strong and determined, indicating that you will continue a career beyond retirement age.

LIFE LINE

- RUNS WIDE AROUND THE THUMB
- WELL-DEVELOPED VENUS MOUNT

You are a "people" person, with a wide circle of friends and interests. Your life line runs straight and clear for most of its length, but becomes fainter with a small fork at around the age of sixty. Normally reflecting a weakening of some type, this looks like a health problem with the lower back. The fork is likely to represent a move, perhaps to an apartment or bungalow. Trauma lines from the teens to the thirties have little effect on the strength of your life line. You are a remarkably resilient person.

Complementary readings

LIFE LINE

LOOP OF VOCATION:
Between your two middle fingers, the loop of vocation displays your commitment to helping people.

MARS POSITIVE MOUNT:
A shallow area in the Mars positive mount shows you have brilliant personnel skills, with the ability to assess people quickly and accurately.

LOOP OF HUMOR:
Between your ring and little fingers, the loop of humor reveals a dry sense of humor.

THUMB TIP:
Your thumb tip has a flattened pad, showing sensitivity to moods. You instinctively know how to make someone happy or sad.

2.4

⋀⋀ LIFE LINE

- ● LINE 'APPEARS' TO BE SHORT
- ● LINE 'APPEARS' TO BE BROKEN

There is often a faint line connecting a short life line to the fate line. Usually this means emigration, with the distance from the life line to the fate line representing the distance of the emigration. Your life line links faintly to your fate line around the age of fifty-five, showing that your career will be the likely cause of your move. With a high start, running close to your thumb, your life line shows that you are an ambitious go-getter who plays your cards close to the vest.

Complementary readings

SUCCESS LINE:
The success line reflecting the higher part of your fate line emphasizes that your career move will be a success.

BASE PHALANX:
The short base phalanx of your little finger reveals a strong desire to belong.

FATE LINE:
Upward branches on your fate line mean a lot of job opportunities. Settling around the age of fifty-five and actually doubling, your fate line shows you will have two careers for a number of years.

⋀⋀ LIFE LINE

VENUS MOUNT:
Your Venus mount is fairly full and rounded, showing vitality for life and love.

THUMB:
Your thumb is fairly rigid, indicating rigidly held ideas.

PALM:
The square, solid palm and shortish fingers reveal you to be naturally cautious.

LIFE LINE

- ● LINE 'APPEARS' TO BE SHORT
- ● LINE 'APPEARS' TO BE BROKEN

Your life line is chained and crossed in the early stages, showing problems and your difficulty in coming to terms with them. In the early twenties, there is a long line linking the life line to the fate line, with the life line growing fainter. In the dominant hand, this is likely to mean emigration, with the distance from the life line to the fate line representing the distance traveled. Beneath the start of your life line is just the start of a double life line, which may indicate a missed opportunity.

Complementary readings

LIFE LINE

CROSS:
The cross on Jupiter mount means that you will achieve your life ambitions.

TRAVEL LINES:
Travel lines show in large numbers on the side of your palm next to the Luna mount.

HEAD LINE:
The writer's fork on your head line, under the ring finger, shows a talent for the written word, with a level, lower fork making you ideal for factual reporting.

FATE LINE:
The fate line running up your palm toward the index finger suggests success in life.

2.6

M LIFE LINE

- SHORT
- HAS A BREAK IN IT

With a break in the life line, you usually see a faint line connecting the life line to the fate line. This often signals emigration, with the distance from your life line to your fate line giving an idea of the distance of the emigration. Sometimes a break represents a radical change of circumstances and living environment. You may, for example, suddenly receive a large fortune.

Complementary readings

FAMILY RINGS:
You have family rings on your little finger and your thumb. The doubling on your thumb suggests a second family home and an inheritance—this could be the early change of circumstances shown by the break.

FATE LINE:
A double start from the Luna mount reveals success, either through a family connection or personal ability.

M LIFE LINE

SUCCESS LINE:
Starting early and running beside your doubled fate line, your success line shows your very promising career prospects.

ANGLE OF TIMING:
The angle of your thumb where it meets your hand shows good timing, with respect to career, business, or music. You may be a highly proficient musician.

LIFE LINE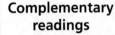

- ● DOUBLE
- ● FULL OR PARTIAL

A double life line denotes your potential to lead a double life, one ordinary and the other probably more challenging and exciting. Many actors, actresses, and show business personalities have this feature. Your second line, running inside the main life line, very deep and close to the thumb, is only developed into your early twenties, indicating that you are not exploiting this second facet of your life. Its depth, however, shows that this second life opportunity is not going to go away.

Complementary readings

HEALTH NOTE: - - - - - - ▶
Exhaustion lines run up your fingers into several fingertips, showing that you lack a natural safety valve to tell you when to take a break.

LIFE LINE

HEAD LINE: - - - - - - - - ▶
Your head line starts high, independently of your life line, showing you to be an adventurous, impulsive, and ambitious risk taker. You are highly motivated and capable of great achievement.

THUMB:
With a long lower phalanx cut around with many resistance rings, you are a very logical, yet highly intuitive person, capable of great perception and foresight.

ᴧᴧ LIFE LINE

- FULL
- FORKED END

After a tough decision in your early to middle fifties, you will emigrate or make a major life change. The clarity and depth of the branch shows your decision to be a good one, despite the fact that the continuing life line is also fairly clear and deep. The fork connects to the fate line, showing that your potential change of country will probably be associated with career progression or advancement. Latticework tying the start of the life line to the head line denotes bouts of both confidence and hesitancy.

Complementary readings

INDEX FINGER:
The island pattern on your index fingertip is usually a sign of success. You will achieve this by being single-minded and by working independently.

JUPITER MOUNT:
Both your index finger and Jupiter mount are dominant, revealing a strongly ambitious individual.

ᴧᴧ LIFE LINE

CROSS:
A cross on your Apollo mount, straddling the success line, suggests financial problems. These will, however, be temporary, as shown by the strength of the success line after the cross.

LINE OF MARS:
Your line of Mars, running inside the life line close to your thumb, is adjacent to the fork, providing protection during what could be a difficult period.

BUSINESS LINE:
This line, branching from your fate line toward your Mercury mount and little finger, indicates the blossoming of strong business links for you.

LIFE LINE

- FULL
- FORKED END

After a tough decision at some point in your sixties, you will emigrate or make a major life change. Both branches of the fork are deep and clear, showing a strong possibility that you will have two very different homes and share time between them.

Complementary readings

FINGERS:
The thick lower phalanxes reveal that you value material wealth.

FATE LINE:
Starting on the Luna mount, your fate line reveals capability. Coupled with a thickset index finger this means you are very ambitious.

HEALTH NOTE:
Double health lines crossing the hand from the middle of the wrist to the little finger show that you need to, and do, take extra care with your health.

HEAD LINE:
A sharply dipping line, together with a short top thumb phalanx, hold you back, undermining the great achievements of which you are capable.

LIFE LINE

VENUS MOUNT:
Your padded mount dominates the rest of your palm, speaking volumes about your need for creature comforts.

⋀⋀ LIFE LINE

● LINE ENDS TUCKED UNDER THE BALL OF THE THUMB

You may be well-traveled, but you always love to return home, and you need to make wherever you are feel like home. Your head line, starting connected to your life line, reinforces a strong attachment to home, and indicates a high degree of sensitivity to the opinions of others. If possible, avoid people who are critical. With an early branch to the Jupiter mount and a branch from the life line to the little finger, you have strong ambition and are especially well-placed for financial success.

Complementary readings

FATE LINE: Starting on the Luna mount, your fate line indicates creative talent. You must use it or it will consume you.

ARTISTIC FLAIR: The curving at the edge of the palm away from the thumb shows artistic flair.

LIFE LINE ⋀⋀

FAMILY RINGS: Family rings around the base of the thumb and little finger reflect the importance of family ties.

LIFE LINE

• LINE ENDS SWEEPING AWAY FROM THE THUMB

You are an adventurous person who enjoys roaming far and wide. Early connecting lines between your life and head lines show both high confidence and self-doubt. As your abilities are confirmed, these branches and anxieties will fade. You have great influence in your personal life and your career, shown by the influence lines in your thirties crossing both the life and fate lines. The lines grow stronger, confirming that your influence has been an asset.

Complementary readings

ATTACHMENT LINE:
Your attachment line breaks but rejoins. If your marriage or partnership suffers an actual separation, it will not last long.

FAMILY RINGS:
Family rings around both the thumb and little finger show the importance you place on home and family. A person who probably travels a great deal for work, you have a greater appreciation of home on your return.

VIA LASCIVIA:
Via lascivia cutting low across the palm on the side opposite to the thumb was historically thought to denote an alcoholic or a drug user. Today, the opposite is true: it shows that you have a high degree of sensitivity, or even allergy, to alcohol and/or drugs of any type.

 LIFE LINE

⋀⋀ LIFE LINE

● LINE STARTS HIGH

You are an ambitious and single-minded individual with a very strong desire to succeed in life. Although crossed lines and chains show early problems, your life line happily becomes clearer and stronger as it proceeds. The life line running close around the thumb, coupled with the thumb naturally held close to the hand, reveal that your are cautious and like control.

SUCCESS LINE:
Mirroring your fate line for most of its length, your success line shows success throughout your career, through recognition, financial reward or promotion. Later in life, the fate and success lines branch, signifying successful self-employment or running of a business.

FATE LINE:
Starting forked, your fate line becomes one strong, flexible line. You start with two careers, gaining success from combining your talents but remaining flexible.

Complementary readings

FATE AND HEAD LINE:
These lines resemble those of a model on international assignments.

⋀⋀ **LIFE LINE**

3.2

LIFE LINE

- ● LINE STARTS LOW
- ● CLOSER TO THE THUMB

You are a content and accepting person, who does not like to cause trouble. Your life line sweeps wide, encompassing a wide circle of family and friends. The fact that the life line starts connected to the head line shows that you enjoy the company and good opinion of others but are not overconcerned. Your hand contains many signs of a natural healer.

Complementary readings

HEALING STRIATA:

Three short lines on the Mercury mount, the healing striata, reveal that you have a talent for putting people at ease. The lines often refer to alternative medicine.

SYMPATHY/EMPATHY LINES:

Sympathy/empathy lines crossing the Jupiter mount show that you care, possibly too deeply. One line means you are ideally suited to the healing and caring professions, multiple lines mean you feel the pain of others.

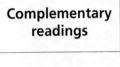 **LIFE LINE**

MERCURY LINE:

The double health line coming from Neptune toward your little finger is the Mercury line which reveals your ability to communicate in a healing way.

VENUS MOUNT:

Your full Venus mount reflects your vitality and general sociability.

3.4

☲ LIFE LINE

- PASSIVE
- DIFFERENCES FROM DOMINANT

There are fairly fundamental differences between your left, passive palm and your right, dominant palm with its double life line. The second, inner life line is undeveloped on your passive hand, indicating a need for security. Also not present in this hand, your potential life map, is a break in your life line. The small part of the double life line that is present is covered with trauma lines, showing how difficult your second life was to achieve. You have overcome a great deal to get to your position in life.

Complementary readings

INDEX FINGER:
A capable and confident person (long index and ring fingers), your slightly bent index finger reveals you to be a little unsure of yourself.

LIFE LINE ☲

HEAD LINE:
Your head line does not start from inside your life line. When you display temper, your inner self does not feel it and is possibly confused by it.

SOLOMON RING:
Absent from the dominant hand, this ring around the base of the index finger shows wisdom, ambition, and leadership, felt as an inner force driving you onward.

NO CURVED LOOP:
The absence of a curved loop on your passive hand suggests that your affinity for water is more of a physical outlet.

LIFE LINE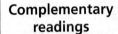

- DOMINANT
- DOUBLE
- FULL OR PARTIAL

Your double life line shows you lead a double life, part mundane and part exciting. This is often present on the hands of actors. A break in the life line in your early twenties shows a time of significant turmoil, with the overlap representing the healing of a broken life. This break comes after a number of trauma lines, indicating difficult incidents. It is only after your early twenties that life settles down and you have smooth sailing.

Complementary readings

FATE LINE:

An early start points to early success and, starting from the Luna mount, shows you excelling in the public arena. You are suited to a career in politics.

HEAD LINE:

Starting just inside the life line, your head line could indicate a belligerent and irascible temper. This is not a sign of willful aggression— you simply tend to attack as the best form of defense.

CURVED LOOP:

A curved loop pattern, below your head line into the Luna mount, shows your strong affinity for water. You may have a home near the sea or a sporting interest involving water. However expressed, water in its many forms makes you come alive.

LIFE LINE

WHO DO YOU LOVE?
HEART LINE

The heart line represents both the physical heart, your feelings, and emotional attitude. All your partnerships, terminated relationships, and love affairs show up on the heart line, as well as experiences involving pain, hurt, and despair. The partners you attract and those you prefer may not be the same ones—if the heart line is different on each hand, you may be attracting a person who is far from your ideal partner. This section describes and illustrates many palms with variations to the heart line.

FIVE COMMONLY ASKED QUESTIONS:

→ Did I choose the right partner?

→ Will I meet my soul mate?

→ In later life, will I be as happy and content with my partner as I am right now?

→ My working life seems to be more important than my love life; will this always be the case?

→ Why do I seem to attract the wrong sort of person?

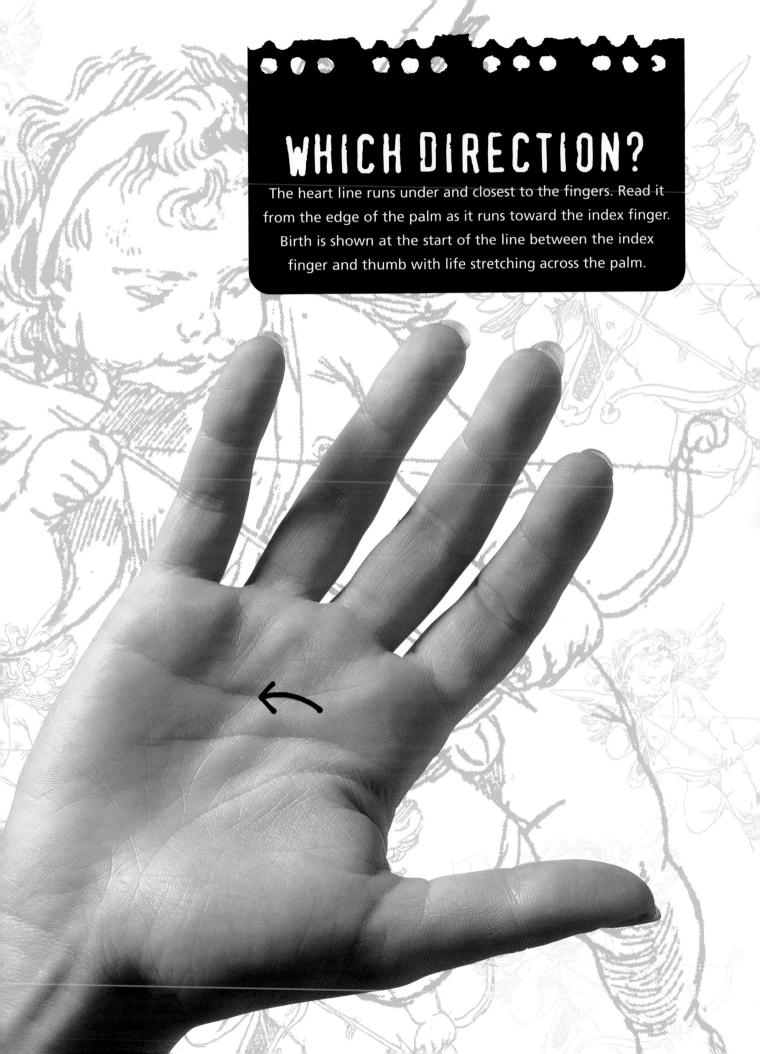

WHICH DIRECTION?

The heart line runs under and closest to the fingers. Read it from the edge of the palm as it runs toward the index finger. Birth is shown at the start of the line between the index finger and thumb with life stretching across the palm.

3.6

♥ HEART LINE

- SHORT
- STRAIGHT
- ENDS UNDER MIDDLE FINGER

Love and romance are important to you but intimacy is possible without love. An intellectually like-minded partner is essential, given your straight heart line. The end of your heart line branching back toward your head line suggests that your head rules your heart: you stand a good chance of becoming a workaholic.

Complementary readings

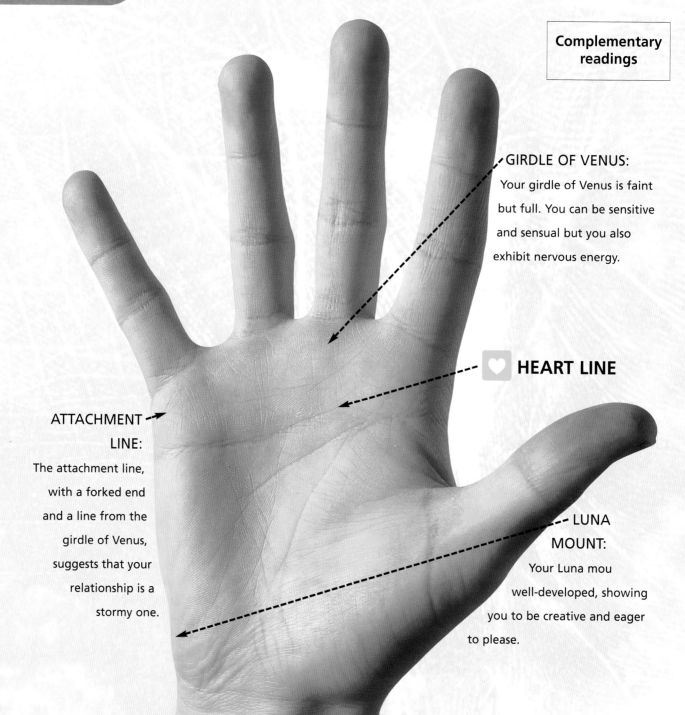

GIRDLE OF VENUS:
Your girdle of Venus is faint but full. You can be sensitive and sensual but you also exhibit nervous energy.

♥ HEART LINE

ATTACHMENT LINE:
The attachment line, with a forked end and a line from the girdle of Venus, suggests that your relationship is a stormy one.

LUNA MOUNT:
Your Luna mou well-developed, showing you to be creative and eager to please.

HEART LINE

- SHORT
- STRAIGHT
- ENDS UNDER MIDDLE FINGER

You have a shrewd, remote, almost businesslike approach to relationships. Although love and romance are important to you, intimacy is possible without love. With your straight heart line, an intellectually like-minded partner is essential.

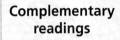

Complementary readings

STARS:

Stars on both your Apollo and Saturn mounts show you achieving excellence and a hard-earned fortune.

ATTACHMENT LINE:

The forked end may indicate a parting of the ways with your partner, or may mean that, although you live together, you lead very separate lives.

SUCCESS LINE:

The line from your success line toward your little finger is known as the business line. Your career is heavily dependent on insight and inspiration for its prosperity.

HEAD LINE:

Your head line springs from your Jupiter mount, showing that drive and aggression easily color your thinking. Starting independently of your life line, it reveals that, as a child, you seek independence, and have a tendency to be impulsive. In maturity, you are a risk taker, and have spectacular failures and successes.

💙 **HEART LINE**

3.8

♡ **HEART LINE**

- **LONG**
- **STRAIGHT**
- **ENDS UNDER THE INDEX FINGER**

You have a strong sense of purpose; you may be a workaholic. This tendency is supported by a horizontal branch from the life line to the heart line. A line running to the index finger from the same point highlights ambition and success. The line slanting slightly toward the Jupiter mount shows you have a romantic side that softens the effect.

Complementary readings

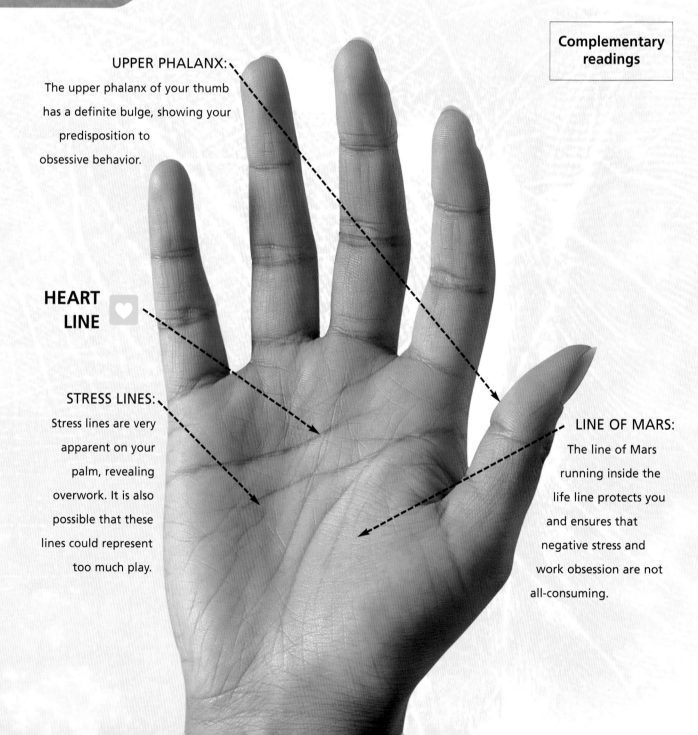

UPPER PHALANX:
The upper phalanx of your thumb has a definite bulge, showing your predisposition to obsessive behavior.

HEART LINE ♡

STRESS LINES:
Stress lines are very apparent on your palm, revealing overwork. It is also possible that these lines could represent too much play.

LINE OF MARS:
The line of Mars running inside the life line protects you and ensures that negative stress and work obsession are not all-consuming.

HEART LINE

- ● ENDS UNDER THE INDEX FINGER
- ● ENDS ON THE JUPITER MOUNT

3.9

This feminine line, found on the hands of both sexes, is both romantic and indicative of emotional vulnerability. Your heart line ends with a branch flicking sharply backward. Known as a kinky flick, this simply means you have an adventurous attitude in relationships. The straightness of the line shows that romance is important to you, but you are not considered a romantic.

Complementary readings

RING OF SOLOMON: The combination of a partial ring of Solomon and a strong index finger shows that you push to take the lead in business dealings.

HEAD LINE: Your long, straight head line shows a practical mentality, with a straightforward, factual, and scientific approach to schemes and ideas. You are ideally suited to a career in information technology, business, or commerce.

PARTIAL GIRDLE OF VENUS: A partial girdle of Venus reflects your earthy sensuality.

HEART LINE

4.0

♥ HEART LINE
● ENDS BETWEEN THE INDEX AND MIDDLE FINGER

This masculine line is a dominant, demanding line. You are a confirmed sensualist, but the branch toward the Jupiter mount shows that you are also capable of romance. In traditional palmistry, the many branches mean that you date or have dated a lot, with each line representing a partner. Today, however, it is considered just as likely that you have just one partner, with the many branches signifying the many different demands you make of him or her. If one person meets all your needs, it will be a sensational partnership.

> **Complementary readings**

APOLLO MOUNT:
Your developed Apollo mount suggests an appreciation of money and a strong sense of fun. People are naturally drawn to you.

FRUSTRATION LINES:
Frustration lines running across your little finger indicate that you have communication difficulties.

HEART LINE ♥

GIRDLE OF VENUS:
A partial girdle of Venus reflects an earthy sensuality and a certain sensitivity.

HEART LINE

● ENDS BETWEEN THE INDEX AND MIDDLE FINGER

You love strongly and deeply, but you express love more with actions than words. The end of your heart line tends toward the base of your index finger, which may show your idealism about partners. You strike a good balance between being too idealistic and too sexual. The many heart line branches either mean a lot of dating, or dating one person but demanding different things from the relationship almost daily.

4.1

Complementary readings

TOP PHALANXES:

Long top phalanxes on your fingers show you are an action person who likes to get on with things. In love, you tend to rush in without fully thinking it through.

HEART LINE

APOLLO MOUNT:

Your well-developed Apollo mount indicates you are open and friendly and attract a lot of people.

MOUNT OF VENUS:

A full, rounded mount of Venus reflects a lovely, warm love life, expressive of healthy physical desires.

4.2

💟 HEART LINE

- ● FORKED END
- ● TRIDENT END

Filled with warmth, idealism, and passion, you have a sensible approach to relationships. The branch of the fork running between the index and middle fingers shows, at its fullest extent, an out-and-out sensualist, but your line stops short of this extreme. The second branch, running straight across your palm, shows a workaholic tendency, but again this line stops short, revealing your fairly serious outlook on relationships.

Complementary readings

💟 HEART LINE

VENUS MOUNT:
Your full mount shows vitality, virility, and sexuality and, as the largest mount of your hand, is the most dominant. These principles are your driving forces.

THUMB:
The top phalanx represents willpower. Your short phalanx denotes a lack of willpower, which, combined with your sensual inquisitiveness and focus on vitality and sexuality, makes you susceptible to temptation. This could give you problems.

HEALTH NOTE:
The top bracelet on your wrist is arched upward, pointing to a weakness in the genitourinary area. Infections are possible, in both men and women.

HEART LINE

- STRONG LINE
- CLEAR LINE

You have a clear, straightforward approach to partnership. A very wide, very deep line suggests a love life that is stuck in a rut. A heart line ending both in the area of the index finger, and between the index and middle fingers, indicates that you have a mixed approach to love and are generally a well-balanced, loving, sensuous, and romantic person.

Complementary readings

HEART LINE

GIRDLE OF VENUS: The girdle of Venus shows the sensual side of your nature.

LEGACY LINE: Springing from an influence line inside the life line, you have a legacy line that runs to the success line. Support and help from your family will bring about your success.

FATE LINE: Your fate line shows you suffering a career setback early in life. Flexibility later in your career give your renewed strength.

VENUS MOUNT: Your Venus mount is well-developed, showing good vitality, sexuality, and libido. Although you will not, of course, feel sexy all the time, you have a definite overall loving outlook.

♥ HEART LINE

● LINE WITH MANY BRANCHES

Either you make diverse demands on your partner on an almost daily basis, or you have dated a great deal. If there has been just one partner, your partnership is a very special one to have stood the test of time and your demands. Ending around the Jupiter mount, your heart line reveals your tendency toward the romantic. The many end branches coming down to the head line indicate that your thoughtfulness is appreciated.

LINE OF MARS:

The line of Mars, the protection and fight back line, is present inside your life line closest to the thumb. You approach any health difficulties with a practical "get on with it" attitude.

Complementary readings

THUMB:

The thumb held close does not look natural. Perhaps lessons you have learned in life have resulted in keeping problems and feelings to yourself.

HEART LINE ♥

HEALTH NOTE:

The extra pattern of dashes over your heart line may point to a potassium deficiency.

INTUITION LINES:

Intuition lines are abundant in the creative and imaginative Luna mount area. You are probably very good at second-guessing.

INTUITION RINGS:

The many rings crossing the base phalanx of your thumb are known as intuition rings.

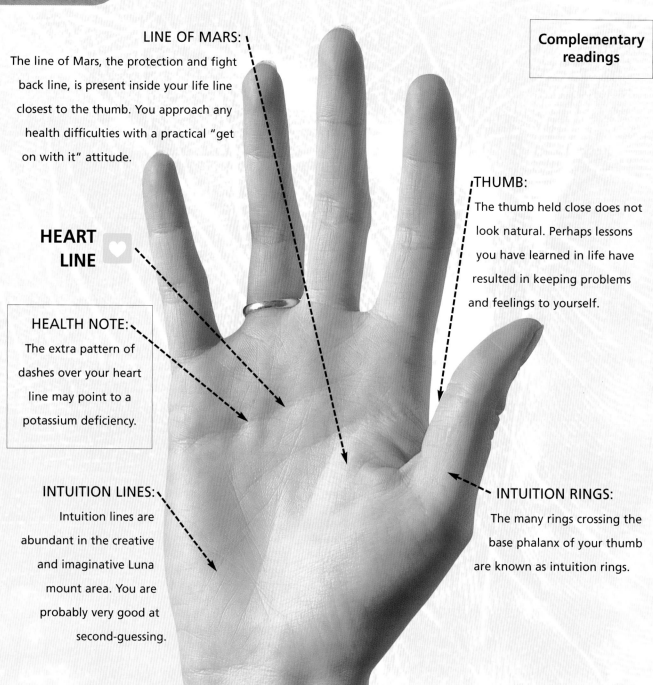

HEART LINE ♡

- DOUBLE
- PARALLEL ANYWHERE

Twice the line means twice the heart. An attractive and loving person, you have a great capacity for love. Your heart line doubles at its end, with the lower, continuous line short and straight, indicating your potential both to love deeply and your susceptibility to fleeting affairs. The upper line ends between your index and middle fingers, which means that the sensual side of your relationships is strongly highlighted.

Complementary readings

FAMILY RINGS:
Rings at the base of your thumb and little finger look like chains with fairly large links, suggesting that you are close to your family.

ATTACHMENT LINES:
Two lines running parallel and close denote two relationships, possibly overlapping. The second line is fainter, showing that a second, conflicting relationship could be avoided if necessary. The second attachment line would be likely to fade over time and even disappear.

THUMB:
Your well-developed top phalanx shows potential for obsessive behavior.

HEART LINE ♡

4.6

♥ HEART LINE

- PASSIVE
- DIFFERENCES FROM DOMINANT

There are fundamental differences between your left, passive palm and your right, dominant palm. On the dominant hand, the passive heart line has a fork running between the fingers, which shows a sensuous stamp on your personality. The second branch runs onto the Jupiter mount but not the finger, showing your inner self to be more romantic than idealistic. The third branch does not appear, indicating that your outward self attracts a different type of person than your inner, vulnerable self desires.

Complementary readings

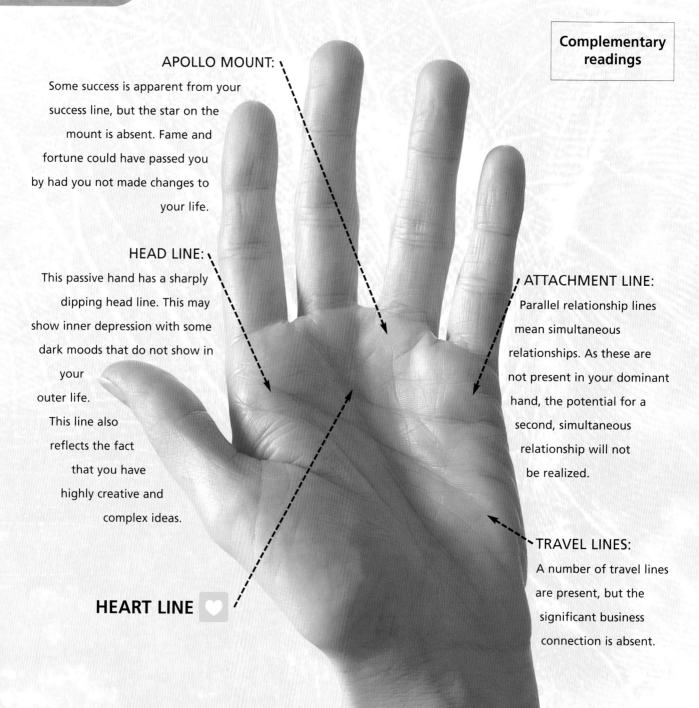

APOLLO MOUNT:

Some success is apparent from your success line, but the star on the mount is absent. Fame and fortune could have passed you by had you not made changes to your life.

HEAD LINE:

This passive hand has a sharply dipping head line. This may show inner depression with some dark moods that do not show in your outer life. This line also reflects the fact that you have highly creative and complex ideas.

HEART LINE ♥

ATTACHMENT LINE:

Parallel relationship lines mean simultaneous relationships. As these are not present in your dominant hand, the potential for a second, simultaneous relationship will not be realized.

TRAVEL LINES:

A number of travel lines are present, but the significant business connection is absent.

HEART LINE

- ● DOMINANT
- ● ENDS ON INDEX FINGER

You have an idealistic approach to relationships, placing your partners on a pedestal. Unless blessed with a truly perfect partner, you are an emotionally vulnerable individual. Your heart line has a faint fork running between the fingers, imposing a sensuous stamp on your personality. The branch leading to your index finger does not travel too far up the finger, revealing curbed idealism. However, the third branch traveling across your hand reflects a workaholic with idealistic tendencies.

4.7

Complementary
readings

HEART LINE

FATE LINE:
Running toward the Jupiter mount, your fate line shows a strong sense of purpose. You are proud and ambitious. There are a number of breaks on the line, but each overlaps, showing your unique skills and versatility.

TRAVEL LINES:
A number of significant journeys are represented on the outer edge of your palm. One particular line meets the success line, indicating a successful business link with a contact in another country or with a foreign person in your own country.

GIRDLE OF VENUS:
A full girdle of Venus shows your sensitivity, compassion, and sensuality. Along with the idealistic aspects of the heart line and stress markings across the hand, the full girdle indicates a degree of nervousness and jumpiness in your character.

STAR:
A star on your Apollo mount signals fame and fortune in the future, earned through hard effort.

ARE YOU INTELLECTUALLY SUPERIOR?

HEAD LINE

The head line represents both the physical head and breadth of intellect and understanding. A sharply dipping line can give a negative aspect to an individual's outlook, but also speaks volumes in terms of potential genius. This section describes and illustrates many palms with variations to the head line.

FIVE COMMONLY ASKED QUESTIONS:

→ What type of career suits me best?

→ Do I have a natural talent as a writer?

→ Am I holding myself back from achieving more?

→ Is ambition part of my nature?

→ Why is it that study seems easier for me than for others?

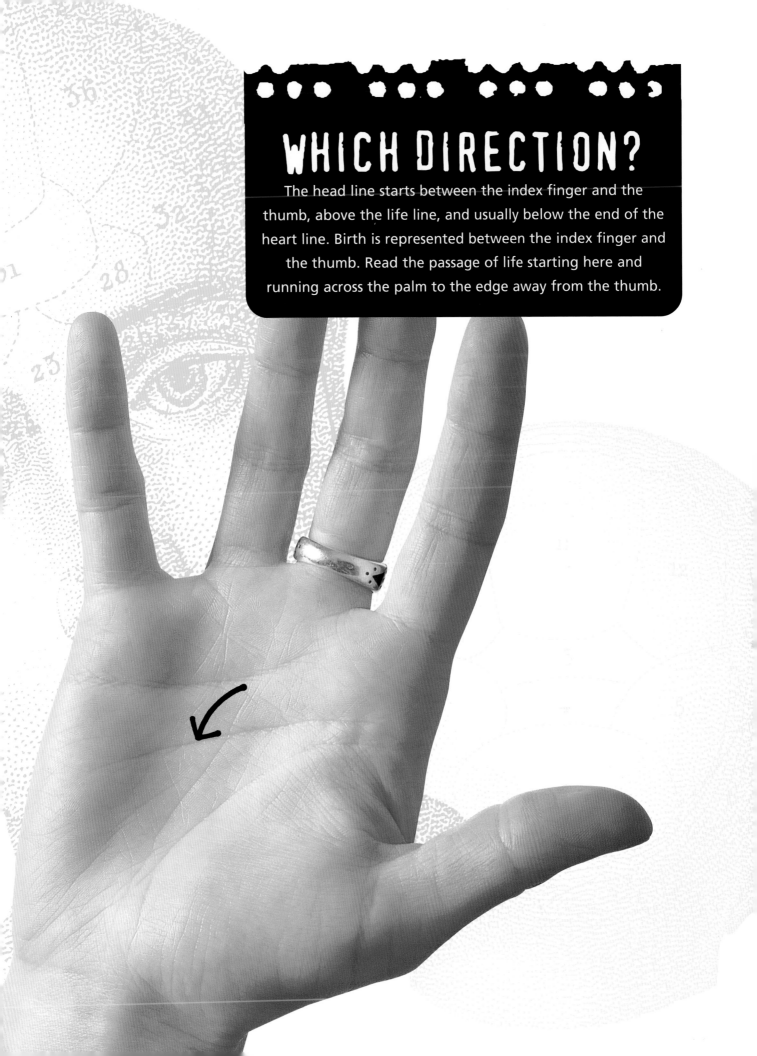

WHICH DIRECTION?

The head line starts between the index finger and the thumb, above the life line, and usually below the end of the heart line. Birth is represented between the index finger and the thumb. Read the passage of life starting here and running across the palm to the edge away from the thumb.

4.8

HEAD LINE

- SHORT
- STRAIGHT
- ENDS UNDER THE MIDDLE FINGER

Perhaps an initiator, you have a desire for security. You are probably a very practical person, good at solving problems. This line is also often found on specialists, such as doctoral students. The outer angle of your lower thumb joint, known as the angle of dexterity, is fairly pronounced, showing both manual and mental dexterity.

Complementary readings

LOOP OF HUMOR:
The loop of humor, between the ring finger and little finger, is well-defined, showing your good, rich sense of fun.

ATTACHMENT LINE:
The attachment line has a faint forked end. There is a strong chance that you will be able to patch up any relationship or marriage difficulties.

HEART LINE:
Your short heart line means that you have a very direct approach to sex and relationships, although the curve shows there is also room for hearts, flowers, and romance.

MOUNT OF VENUS:
A full, rounded mount of Venus denotes a lovely, warm, love life expressing healthy physical desires. Open and friendly, you attract a lot of people with your witty and charming personality.

HEAD LINE

HEAD LINE

- ● LONG
- ● STRAIGHT LINE
- ● ENDS UNDER THE RING OR MIDDLE FINGER

You have a very practical mentality and are ideally suited to science, technology, business, and commerce. This head line is actually known as a Sydney line and suggests some of the fierce intensity and focus associated with the simian line. Your fate line, directed to the index finger, points to a strong managerial focus to your career. You have a good chance of success in this field, but at a price: you have many negative stress lines.

Complementary readings

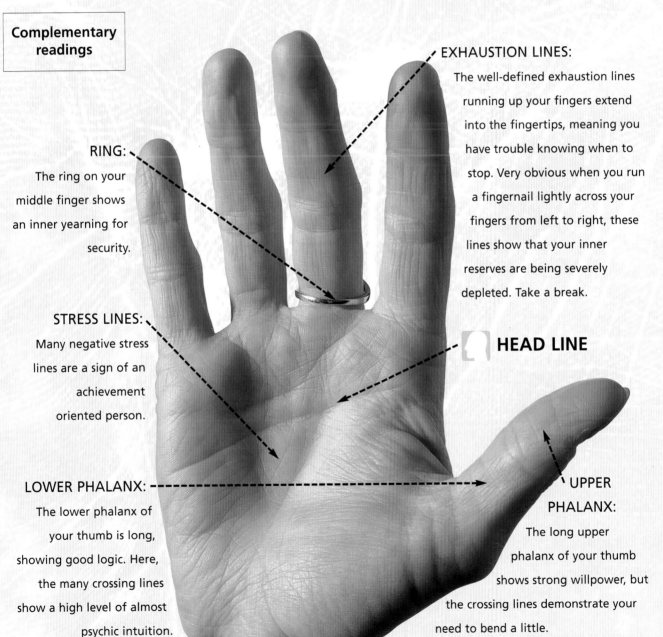

EXHAUSTION LINES:
The well-defined exhaustion lines running up your fingers extend into the fingertips, meaning you have trouble knowing when to stop. Very obvious when you run a fingernail lightly across your fingers from left to right, these lines show that your inner reserves are being severely depleted. Take a break.

RING:
The ring on your middle finger shows an inner yearning for security.

HEAD LINE

STRESS LINES:
Many negative stress lines are a sign of an achievement oriented person.

LOWER PHALANX:
The lower phalanx of your thumb is long, showing good logic. Here, the many crossing lines show a high level of almost psychic intuition.

UPPER PHALANX:
The long upper phalanx of your thumb shows strong willpower, but the crossing lines demonstrate your need to bend a little.

HEAD LINE
- LONG
- CURVES DOWNWARD

The head line ends on the mount of Luna, indicating a creative and artistic talent. Your head line starts independently of your life line, showing independence from an early age. You are an adventurous risk-taker. The latticework of lines connecting the start of your head line to your life line reveals bursts of confidence alternating with withdrawals into self-doubt. These lines appear fairly faint, suggesting that you are overcoming self-doubt by a healthy appreciation of your own talents.

Complementary readings

ISLANDS:
The island patterns on the fingertips of your index and ring fingers signify success, both in the domain of business and ambition and in the domain of fun and pleasure.

SUCCESS LINE:
Your success line comes into its own on your Apollo mount, clearly showing public recognition. Considering your fate line, real recognition and satisfaction will probably not come solely from a conventional job.

HEAD LINE

WHORL:
A palmar ridge whorl, such as this one on your Luna mount, shows a special gift or talent. It can also signal a heartfelt desire to fulfill yourself creatively. Write that novel or paint that masterpiece.

FATE LINE:
Your career has an uncertain start, settling into job satisfaction in your twenties. A period of self-employment in your late forties or fifties provides some success.

HEAD LINE

- ● LONG
- ● SHARPLY DIPPING

You are imaginative with melancholic tendancies if suppressed. This is the thin line between genius and madness. Your curved head line running deep into the Luna mount shows that, with your great power of imagination, you are not entirely materialistic in your ideas. This line shows that you have the essential qualities needed for translating, public speaking, or writing. Trusting feelings implicitly is second nature to you, and behavior perceived by others as irrational often gets surprising results.

Complementary readings

HEAD LINE

LITTLE FINGER:
Your little finger stands apart, denoting independence of thought. You will probably enter a creative or artistic profession or be the leader of an organization.

AMBITION LINE:
The short line running from your life line to your Jupiter mount is known as an ambition line, and shows that you will achieve your ambitions. These are likely to be academic ambitions, such as passing an examination.

HEALTH NOTE:
A particularly low freckle on your hand could point to a copper deficiency, especially if it has not always been there.

HEAD LINE

• STARTS CONNECTED TO THE LIFE LINE

You are often more cautious and careful than is warranted, tending to measure yourself by what others think of you. Despite being straight and strong, your head line remains connected to your life line for some distance, showing a lack of confidence or self-assurance. You should generally try to avoid negative and overcritical people. Sufficient talent and strong qualities will eventually help to reassure you, but your major achievements are often the result of wanting to prove yourself over and over again.

Complementary readings

GIRDLE OF VENUS:
The girdle of Venus shows a strong possibility that you are overemotional.

HEAD LINE

LINE OF MARS:
Your line of Mars, the guardian angel line, shows that you are able to spring back and pick up the pieces when life gets you down.

FATE LINE:
Your fate line starts very close to your life line. Together with the tied head and life lines, this shows your strong link to family members and their opinions, or suggests that you will do well in a family profession.

BASE PHALANX:
The base phalanx of your thumb is long, indicating that you have a logical nature.

TOP PHALANX:
The long top phalanx of your thumb shows willpower to help you overcome any feelings of inadequacy.

HEAD LINE

• START COMPLETELY SEPARATE FROM THE LIFE LINE

You have always been strongly independent, even in childhood. Likely to be an adventurous and impulsive risk taker, you may inspire criticism for being too outspoken. Your unpredictable approach to projects can sometimes work spectacularly and at other times can be your undoing. The combination of your short, top thumb phalanx, denoting low willpower, and your very long ring finger indicates your susceptibility to excessive gambling. It is worth noting that it is not just money that can be gambled.

Complementary readings

HEAD LINE

ISLAND:
An island fingerprint pattern on your index finger is a good sign of success, but this is more likely to be achieved working alone than as part of a team.

VIA LASCIVIA:
Once interpreted as a lascivious, overindulgent marking, via lascivia is more correctly interpreted today as a sign of allergies or of sensitivity to alcohol or painkillers, even in the smallest quantities.

HEAD LINE:
The upward fork on your head line points to strong business knowledge and acumen, which, together with a strong index finger, could be your saving grace.

5.4

HEAD LINE

- LINE STARTS HIGH
- CLOSER TO THE INDEX FINGER THAN THE THUMB

Highly motivated and capable of great achievements, you are by nature ambitious. The start of your head line is separate from your life line, denoting your independence. You know your own mind and are also potentially a risk taker. The strong, deep, and clear head line shows clarity of thought applied in a straightforward and logical way.

ARCH:
An arch fingerprint pattern on the index finger shows a strong sense of wanting to protect and secure everyone and everything around you. This urge is likely to be an active part of your personality.

Complementary readings

LOOP OF HUMOR:
Though you are charming and friendly, the combination of a loop of humor, between the ring and little fingers, and a developed Venus mount, makes you positively magnetic.

HEAD LINE

HEART LINE:
Ending on the index finger, your heart line shows a tendency to idealize partnerships. This is a possible reason for the number of negative stress lines on your palm.

TOP PHALANX:
The top phalanx of your thumb reveals a lot of willpower, with the backward flex showing a wide circle of friends.

HEAD LINE

- **STARTS LOW**
- **CLOSER TO THE THUMB THAN THE INDEX FINGER**

5.5

A head line very close to the thumb indicates that you may have low self-esteem and a strong temper. Misunderstood, you tend to use attack as the best form of defense. Although your life line starts low, showing calm and acceptance, your long head line, known as a Sydney line, reflects your fiery intensity, focus, and determination, very much like a simian line. A line of courage cuts across the palm from just above the thumb as a sign of bravery and a willingness to stand up for your principles.

Complementary readings

HEAD LINE

FATE LINE:
Your fate line is flexible and changes direction, reflecting career changes within an organization rather than between companies. The clarity and depth of the line shows you are someone who changes direction when your career doesn't go as planned.

SUCCESS LINE:
The success line springing from Mars negative translates as success coming from your professionalism and integrity.

HEALTH NOTE:
The cracked pattern of negative stress over your palm could, in part, be because of your type of head line pushing you onward.

5.6

HEAD LINE

• ENDS IN AN UPWARD FORK

You have strong business acumen and a feel for successful business practices. Your head line itself is wavy, patchy in places, and has an island, which usually indicates a time of weakness. Your mind is easily distracted. The lightly etched appearance of the line suggests that thinking deeply or studying is a strain. This seems to be caused, in your case, by ill health, shown by the island and by other similarly affected lines.

MERCURY LINE:
The line running from your Venus mount diagonally across your palm to your little finger is the Mercury or health line, indicating that you should take care of your health.

Complementary readings

LIFE LINE:
Four episodes of trauma are evident in the health related trauma lines that show as patches on your life line. The last period of trauma seems to be in your early thirties, when your life hits a long, clear spell.

HEAD LINE

VIA LASCIVIA:
The via lascivia, or allergies line, is a deep line across your palm from the edge opposite the thumb. In such a potentially sensitive palm, this may mean you develop allergies to previously tolerated drugs.

HEAD LINE

● ENDS IN A DOWNWARD FORK

Known as a writer's fork if the branching is below the ring finger, this downward fork denotes a commercially successful creative talent. The branch is fairly level and does not dip too sharply, which suggests nonfiction creative writing. Your head line starts independently of the life line but is tied to it with a latticework of branching lines. This shows that, although independent, you are alternately confident and hesitant, a trait which can be overcome if your life and head lines run parallel for no more than an inch.

Complementary readings

DROPLETS:

Droplets on all fingertips show exceptional sensitivity. A rare sign of extraordinary talent, legend has it that with this gift you can "feel" colors.

FATE LINE:

Starting from the Venus mount inside the life line, your fate line tells of early family commitments. You are possibly a parent wanting success through or for your children. A radical change in your thirties brings a new career direction.

TEACHER'S SQUARE:

The teacher's square on your Jupiter mount reveals a talent for instruction on almost any subject.

JUPITER MOUNT:

A strong index finger and developed Jupiter mount show that ambition is strongly highlighted for you.

STAR:

The star on your Apollo mount shows that you will achieve fame and fortune.

HEAD LINE

5.8

HEAD LINE

● LINE HAS A TRIDENT END

You have extraordinary mental abilities. Business acumen, determination, and inspiration are your recipe for success. The branch to Mars negative, on the outer edge of your palm, shows determination and fortitude, the branch to Luna mount shows inspiration and creativity, and the small branch deep into the Luna mount shows a complex imagination.

Complementary readings

STAR:
A star on your Apollo mount is a reliable sign of fame and fortune.

SOLOMON RING:
A small Solomon ring on the base of your index finger denotes a natural aptitude for leadership and responsibility. Often people with this marking are pushed by others to lead because they do not seek leadership positions themselves.

HEAD LINE

FATE LINES:
Double fate lines could mean you have two careers running side by side, or of undertaking prospect-enhancing study part-time while working.

BRANCH:
The branch from your life line to your Saturn mount is an unusual feature and shows a massive, ultimately successful, effort to achieve something of major importance to you.

HEAD LINE

- DOUBLE
- PART OR FULL

A sure sign of brainpower, the double head line is seen here as part of a pseudo-simian line. A double head line is normally interpreted by combining the qualities of each individual line. Your upper line curves gently down toward the Luna mount, showing a creative predisposition. Your lower line is straight, directed toward the outer edge of the palm, showing a logical intellect. You are capable both of great turmoil and massive achievement.

Complementary readings

BLUE NAIL POLISH:
Blue nail polish could mean that you have an attraction to the mystical realm.

HEAD LINE

TEACHER'S SQUARE:
You have a teacher's square on your Jupiter mount that looks like a diamond, as it stands on a point. Also present on teachers and tutors who love their occupation, this sign shows you have a real gift for teaching almost any subject, when you have attentive pupils who want to learn.

HEAD LINE

- **LONG**
- **SHARPLY DIPPING LINE**

You have a great imagination, which if suppressed, could lead to depression. With the head line deep in your Luna mount, you are prone to hypersensitivity and must use your creative energies, otherwise they are likely to consume you. Your clear, long head line shows clarity of vision. Bridging lines at the start of your life line express confidence with periods of self-doubt. A common-sense appreciation of talent will cause this latticework to fade over time.

Complementary readings

PALMAR RIDGE:
A tri-radii palmar ridge pattern on the Mercury and Jupiter mounts gives intensity to these areas. Communication and leading innovation are strongly highlighted for you.

HEAD LINE

ATTACHMENT LINE:
Your attachment line has a fork with an exceptionally long, continuing branch, suggesting a soul mate.

HEART LINE:
Your heart line ends strongly on the index finger, showing that you idealize partners. A lesser branch falling back to the life line reflects the intensity you give your life's work.

TOP PHALANX:
The tapered top phalanx of your thumb shows sensitivity to moods, people, and emotions.

HEAD LINE

- • DOMINANT HAND
- • PASSIVE HAND - DIFFERENCES

There are fundamental differences between these right and left hands. While the left palm shows a long head line dipping into the Luna mount, the right hand head line has branches to Mars negative. On the passive hand, this means inner determination. A branch from the life line through the start of the head line shows that you are destined for success, with the loop of inspiration on your Luna mount reflecting an excess of talent.

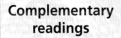

Complementary readings

LIFE LINE:
A double life line on this passive hand, faint but present, means that you have the potential for a very different life. This alternative life has not been followed as it does not appear in the dominant left hand, which represents current, actual life.

ATTACHMENT LINES:
Attachment lines show up as two long lines, revealing the possibility of soul mate partners. The second partner will not materialize, as there is just one partner shown in the dominant hand.

HEAD LINE

WHAT DOES THIS UNIQUE HAND MARKING MEAN?

SIMIAN LINE

The simian line appears as a line cutting straight across the palm, from between the thumb and index finger across to the outer edge, and is actually a head and heart line fused together.

A simian line is often, though not exclusively, associated with Down's syndrome. When seen in a non-Down's syndrome hand, it signifies extraordinary intensity and powers of achievement. A simian line indicates a very focused and forceful person who is an excellent achiever, but someone who has difficulty relating emotionally. Einstein was rumored to have a simian line. Possessiveness and jealousy in relationships can be a problem for such individuals. The presence of a head and/or heart line softens some of the characteristics of the simian line and it is then known as a pseudo-simian line.

FIVE COMMONLY ASKED QUESTIONS:

→ Why do I have to do everything perfectly?

→ Why do I feel different from others?

→ If I don't have a heart line, does it mean I am unfeeling or will be unlucky in love?

→ Will I achieve what I set out to do?

→ Will I always live my life with such intensity?

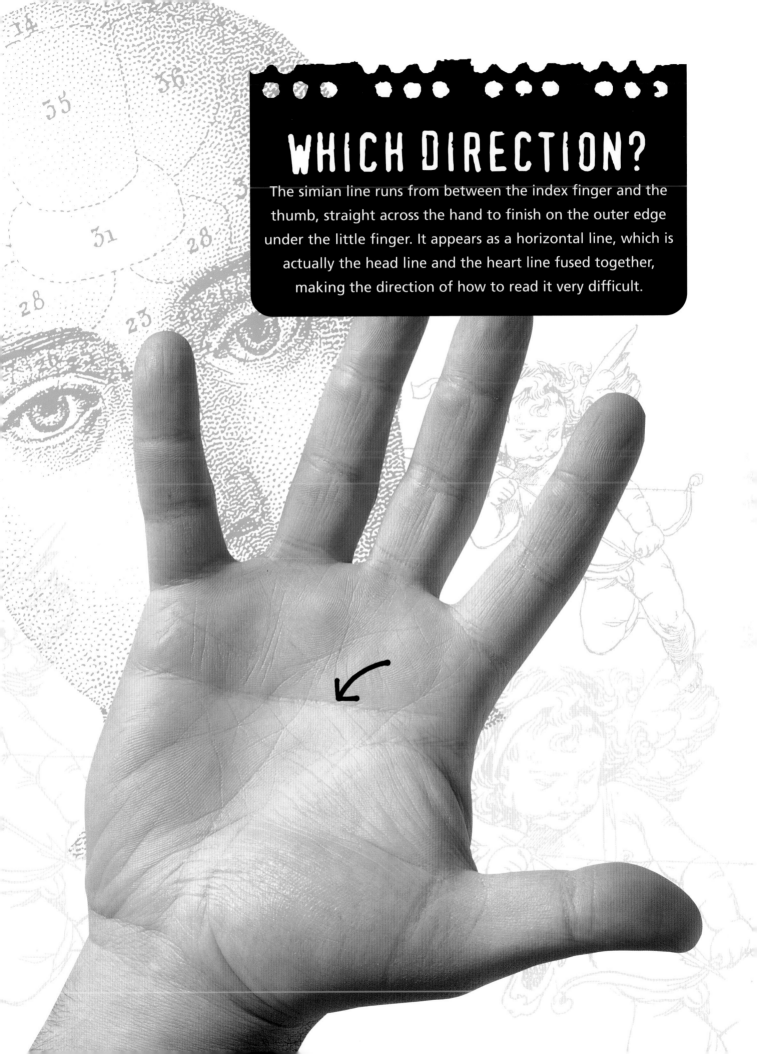

WHICH DIRECTION?

The simian line runs from between the index finger and the thumb, straight across the hand to finish on the outer edge under the little finger. It appears as a horizontal line, which is actually the head line and the heart line fused together, making the direction of how to read it very difficult.

6.2

SIMIAN LINE

- STRAIGHT ACROSS PALM
- NO HEAD LINE
- NO HEART LINE

You are an individual whose concentrated mental energies are applied with laserlike intensity, you simply cannot be disturbed when absorbed in a task. You are essentially a major achiever. A heavily chained simian line tells of difficulties in your life. The fate line extending to your index finger points to success in business, with the long top phalanx of your thumb indicating great willpower and determination.

Complementary readings

SYMPATHY/ EMPATHY LINES:
Many sympathy / empathy lines show you care deeply.

LIFE LINE:
Your apparently short life line with a line connecting to the fate line points to an emigration early in life after some trauma. The clarity of the continuing line means your life gets easier.

STRESS LINES:
Negative stress lines cover your hand, including exhaustion lines up the fingers. These can be controlled, though with your determination to see a project through, they are likely to return again and again.

GIRDLE OF VENUS:
A full girdle of Venus shows the sensitivity, compassion, and sensuality in your nature. A coiled spring, you have an abundance of nervous energy, as illustrated by the branched appearance.

SIMIAN LINE

SIMIAN LINE

- WITH HEART LINE
- WITH HEAD LINE

6.3

Intensity and concentrated mental energies that are never applied halfheartedly are your trademarks. You dislike being disturbed when absorbed in a task, which usually results in successful completion of the task. You prefer one task at a time. A major achiever, your heart and head lines soften a potentially hard approach to other people and ideas.

Complementary readings

ISLAND

FINGERPRINTS:

This pattern on all your fingers is a major sign that you are someone who will be or is extremely successful. Combined with the simian nature of your hand, these fingertips reveal a truly indomitable character.

MERCURY LINE:

This line, starting from your Venus mount and sweeping toward your little finger, is usually a health warning of some kind. It cuts across an early fate line, allowing a second fate line from the Luna mount to take over.

HEAD LINE:

Starting linked to your life line by a pattern of latticework, your head line shows spurts of confidence followed by periods of self-doubt. Self-assurance will go a long way toward negating these feelings. If the negative feelings are overcome, these lines will fade in time.

SIMIAN LINE

6.4

 SIMIAN LINE

- STRAIGHT ACROSS THE HAND
- NO HEART OR HEAD LINES
- PASSIVE
- SAME ON BOTH HANDS

You apply concentrated mental energies with laserlike intensity. Never halfhearted, you simply cannot be disturbed when absorbed in a task. You are likely to be extremely gifted intellectually. With simian lines on both hands, the effects are multiplied, making you extremely successful.

Complementary readings

SIMIAN LINE

AMBITION LINE:
The line coming from the life line toward the Jupiter mount shows successful completion of a heartfelt ambition.

LIFE LINE:
Your life line has a slightly difficult start, but this passive hand shows fewer obstacles than in your dominant hand, revealing a more awkward but ultimately exciting path in life.

MYSTIC CROSS:
The mystic cross highlights a highly developed intuition which can mean a talent for speculative business deals.

MERCURY LINE:
This branch line, from your life line to your little finger, shows a health issue that needs attention. On your dominant hand, however, this line appears as a business line coming from the fate line.

FATE LINE:
Rising branches on this line means that you will become self-employed.

SIMIAN LINE

- **STRAIGHT ACROSS THE HAND**
- **NO HEART OR HEAD LINES**
- **DOMINANT**

You are highly focused. Sometimes indicating Down's syndrome, this is also the mark of a major achiever. You are likely to be extremely gifted intellectually. The simian line is thought to be formed by a fusion of the head and heart lines, giving you the potential to be totally self-centered and subjective in your dealings. You have a strong need for secure material foundations.

Complementary readings

SIMIAN LINE

AMBITION LINE:

This line that moves from the life line toward the Jupiter mount shows success in a lifelong ambition.

LIFE LINE:

Your life line has a difficult start with a number of crossing lines in childhood. Trauma lines scattered throughout your life keep you on your toes but do not bowl you over. A fork in your line around the age of forty shows an emigration or major change following a tough decision.

FATE LINE:

A significant opportunity in your forties causes a change in career direction, shown by the change in line direction. The doubled line and the stars on the main line light the way for change and help you to shine.

MERCURY LINE:

A branch line from the fate line to the little finger shows that success in your career depends on insight and inspiration.

ARE YOU IN THE RIGHT CAREER?
FATE LINE

The fate line gives information about your career, how you feel about it, and whether it is challenging you. A straight, clear, deep line indicates a long and successful career. A line that stops and starts, running clearly, then faintly, shows career twists and turns. A line cutting clearly across the fate line may indicate that you are being searched out for a specific job. This section describes and illustrates many palms with variations to the fate line.

FIVE COMMONLY ASKED QUESTIONS:

→ Did I choose the right career?

→ Will I be head-hunted?

→ Will I achieve my ambition of working for myself?

→ My working life seems to be constantly changing; will it settle down in the future?

→ Should I take up an new, exciting career that is being offered to me?

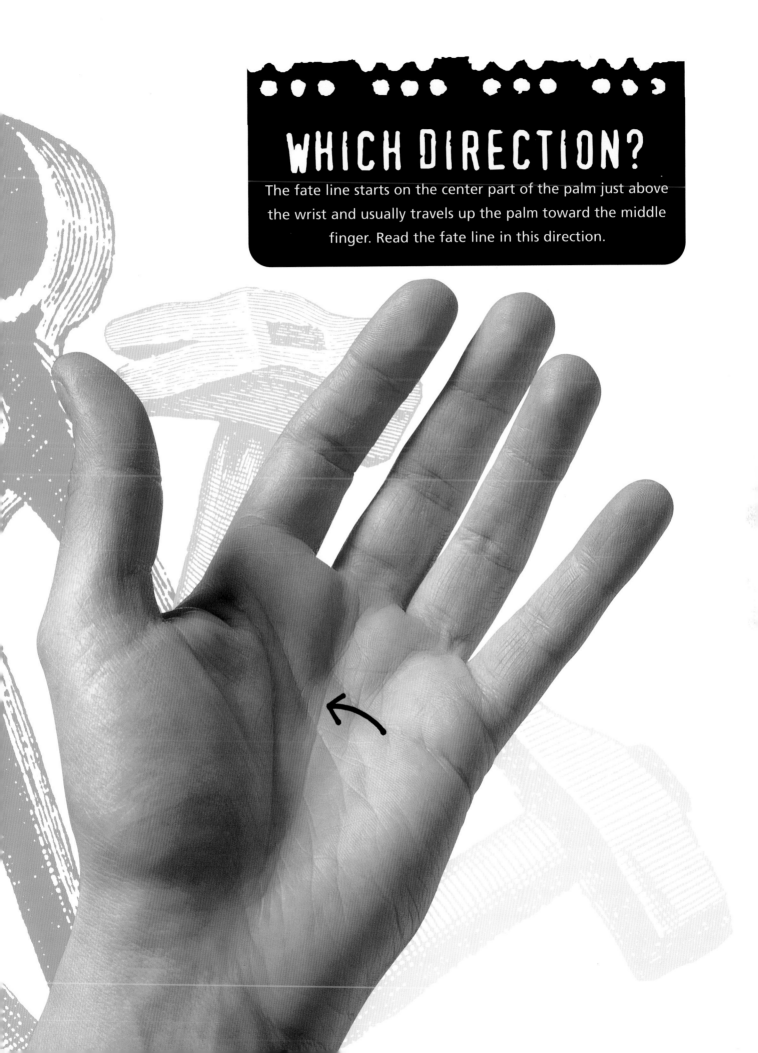

WHICH DIRECTION?

The fate line starts on the center part of the palm just above the wrist and usually travels up the palm toward the middle finger. Read the fate line in this direction.

FATE LINE

- STRAIGHT LINE
- CLEARLY DEFINED LINE

Probably someone who has always known what you wanted to be, you have a strong, vocational, job-for-life line. A possible new career opportunity, shown as a rising branch, appears in your twenties. The new job is not pursued as the line does not change direction, but your continuing career appears much stronger and more fulfilling. Your index finger is very thick, showing natural leadership and business sense, with your little finger held apart denoting independence of thought.

6.6

Complementary readings

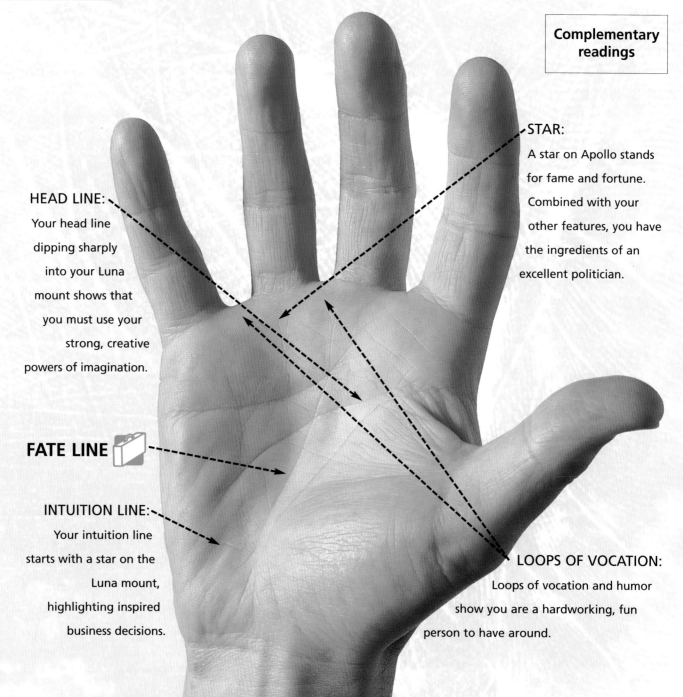

HEAD LINE:
Your head line dipping sharply into your Luna mount shows that you must use your strong, creative powers of imagination.

FATE LINE

INTUITION LINE:
Your intuition line starts with a star on the Luna mount, highlighting inspired business decisions.

STAR:
A star on Apollo stands for fame and fortune. Combined with your other features, you have the ingredients of an excellent politician.

LOOPS OF VOCATION:
Loops of vocation and humor show you are a hardworking, fun person to have around.

FATE LINE

• LINE APPEARS TO STOP AND START

6.7

You will have numerous changes of career or employer, due in many cases to boredom, frustration, or lack of challenges. The girdle of Venus adds nervous energy to your need to change direction. A heart line branch thrown downward to the head line acts like a simian line, pushing you with intensity to focus on new challenges. This may have the result of turning you into a workaholic or a nervous wreck.

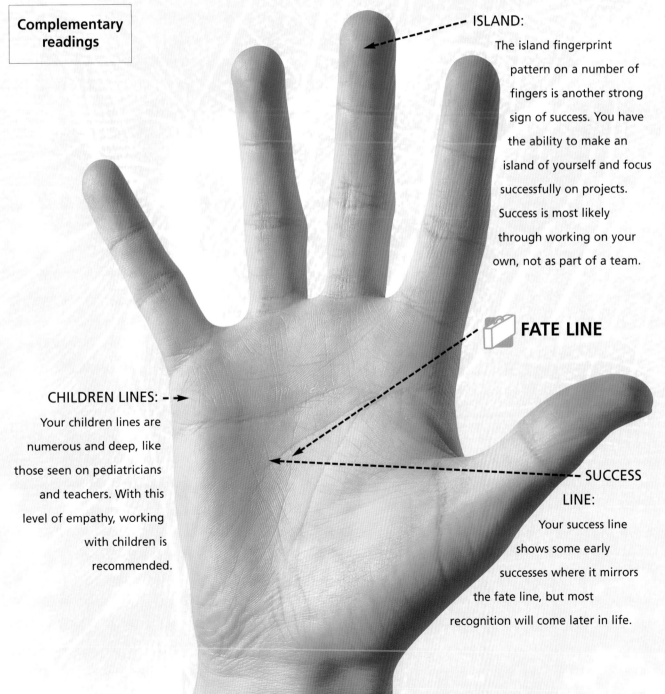

Complementary readings

ISLAND:
The island fingerprint pattern on a number of fingers is another strong sign of success. You have the ability to make an island of yourself and focus successfully on projects. Success is most likely through working on your own, not as part of a team.

FATE LINE

CHILDREN LINES:
Your children lines are numerous and deep, like those seen on pediatricians and teachers. With this level of empathy, working with children is recommended.

SUCCESS LINE:
Your success line shows some early successes where it mirrors the fate line, but most recognition will come later in life.

6.8

 FATE LINE

● STARTS HIGH ON THE PALM

You will only start a career, or begin to feel secure in your chosen career, later in life. There are actually two fate lines visible, with the shorter one starting in your thirties and ending around the age of fifty. This line, rather than representing a second career, thwarts aims and ambitions along its length. The main career line, to the left of the shortened line, suffers some faintness and changing of direction while the shorter line is active. Later in life, when you enjoy some success, the success line mirrors the main fate line.

Complementary readings

TRAUMA LINES:
Many trauma lines cross the life line until the mid-thirties, when your life seems to become more comfortable.

 FATE LINE

LIFE LINE:
Your double life line is fairly developed and similar in appearance to a line often seen on actors. In thespian terms, the double life represents home life and life on stage or screen.

VIA LASCIVIA:
The via lascivia is fairly prominent on the lower part of your Luna mount. The hand itself is fairly delicate in appearance, with a stress patterning of fine lines. Any substances causing allergy or sensitivity should probably be avoided.

FATE LINE

● STARTS IN THE LUNA MOUNT

A career in the limelight or in politics would be the most suitable one for you. Palmists often have difficulty when interpreting hands full of stress lines, like this one, in picking out the main lines as clearly as possible. Your fate line is very deep and clear, running straight from the Luna mount to the index finger. In your potential career in the limelight, this indicates elements of pride and ambition, as well as a natural desire to promote yourself.

6.9

Complementary readings

INFLUENCE LINES:
Two significant influence lines, one in your twenties and another in your fifties, run across your life line to the Mercury mount, showing you as strong and positive, open to opportunities for self-promotion in the media.

RING OF SOLOMON:
The Ring of Solomon around the base of your index finger shows a natural talent for leadership.

ULNAR LOOPS:
Ulnar loops on all the fingers show your versatility and adaptability in wide-ranging situations.

HEART LINE:
Your short, straight, level heart line indicates that your partners know exactly where they stand in your life.

FATE LINE

7.0

 FATE LINE

● STOPS FAR SHORT BEFORE THE BASE OF THE FINGERS

Your fate line stops short at the heart line, indicating that you may experience a sudden fortunate change in circumstances, perhaps a lottery win or a chance windfall. Other characteristics in your palm reinforce this: there seem to be a lot of pointers to a possible lucky change of lifestyle.

Complementary readings

STAR:

A star on your Apollo mount is a strong indication of fame and fortune.

HEAD LINE:

Your head line ends in a long fork, with a branch to Mars negative highlighting determination and perseverance and a branch to Luna mount showing creativity.

LIFE LINE:

The early portion of your life line shows some disturbances, but it becomes much clearer from the thirties onward. A fork shows a major change in circumstance or an emigration around the end of the fate line, with a branch to the little finger at the same point showing a clearer business focus.

 FATE LINE

FATE LINE

- ● ENDS HIGH ON THE PALM
- ● STOPS AT THE BASE OF THE FINGERS

You will either work, probably voluntarily, past retirement age or become engrossed in a retirement occupation. A fate line starting early and continuing all the way to the base of the fingers is always a sign of driving life energy. Your clear, strong fate line suggests that your job is fulfilling and challenging in its own right, and that you enjoy a high degree of success.

Complementary readings

FATE LINE

MOUNT OF JUPITER:
A very developed mount of Jupiter shows that you are highly ambitious.

MARS POSITIVE:
Mars positive has the appearance of a shallow lake, denoting your ability to assess people quickly and accurately.

VENUS MOUNT:
Your well-developed Venus mount reinforces how important it is for you to maintain working contacts with people.

HEAD LINE:
Your head line ends in a writer's fork below the ring finger, a sign that you will derive a lot of pleasure from the occupation of writing.

FATE LINE

● ENDS TOWARD THE INDEX FINGER

With natural ambition, pride, and self-promotion, you are likely to achieve great success. Your double fate line paints a picture of you working at your success, with the main career line going straight to and ending right on the Jupiter mount. Your success is guaranteed and will be earned through your own efforts.

Complementary readings

LOOP OF INSPIRATION: The loop of inspiration on the Luna mount is the element that transforms you from a good person into a great one.

 FATE LINE

HEAD LINE: A second straight, clear head line shows that you have a balanced and clear perspective on a variety of issues.

TRAVEL LINES: Many travel lines are present next to the Luna mount, one of which extends to the fate line, representing regular dealings with a business contact in another country.

FATE LINE

- **LINE WITH A LINE STRIKING IT**
- **UPWARD JOINING BRANCH**

The upward branch is a good indication of a positive career move. Two opportunities appear in your thirties, with the earlier one crossing the fate line without being pursued. This first branch, going toward the Mercury mount, is the business line, showing that you have a strong edge in commercial dealings. The stock market is full of people with business lines. The career opportunity branch changes the direction of the fate line slightly.

Complementary readings

ISLAND:

Island fingerprint patterns on your ring and little fingers show great achievements in the world of money, fun, and communications.

LOOPS OF VOCATION:

Loops of vocation and humor show that you have a lovely, rounded personality.

RAJAH LOOP:

A Rajah loop present between the index and middle fingers is both rare and significant. You may have a direct blood connection to royalty, and are likely to have a regal attitude and refined tastes.

FATE LINE

SUCCESS LINE:

Your success line does not, oddly enough, mirror the fate line, showing that success and recognition in your life appear to come from entirely different angles.

LIFE LINE:

A branch from the life line shooting to the Jupiter mount points to ambition and success.

7.4

FATE LINE

• STARTS ON VENUS MOUNT

Your career is probably tied in some way to your family. In addition to the one on the Venus mount, your fate line has a number of other starts, which combine into one line and career around your late twenties or early thirties. Multiple starter branches usually signify courses of study combined with career. This palm is not so simple. With your multiple lines, you are likely to have many strings to your bow and be capable of pursuing many jobs successfully.

Complementary readings

BRANCH FROM FATE LINE:
A partially double life line points to a second, exciting, and successful career that you will take up in the future.

A branch from the center of your palm straight to the Jupiter mount shows leadership talents and business success.

SUCCESS LINE:
Your success line, sweeping from the Luna mount and running parallel to the main fate line, shows a successful career with a good degree of public exposure and recognition.

FATE LINE

FATE LINE

● MULTIPLE ENDS

7.5

Multiple fate lines reflect the running of several careers at the same time. Just after crossing your head line, sometime in your fifties, your fate line breaks into a number of lines. You will probably enter a period of self-employment or run a business, undertaking multiple roles yourself. The strength of the lines suggests business success. The continuation of the central line or role, and the success lines, reinforce this pattern.

Complementary readings

AMBITION LINES:
Running upward from the start of the life line are two ambition or achievement lines. These represent lifelong academic ambitions that have been or will be achieved.

JUPITER MOUNT:
Your well-developed Jupiter mount shows that you focus on ambition, pride, leadership, and honor. You believe in your own worth, but as the mount is not overdeveloped, you are also fully aware of your faults.

FATE LINE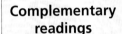

BUSINESS LINE:
Peeling from the lower part of the life line and running toward the little finger is a business line, or Mercury line. The growth and success of your career or business depends on a business sixth sense to keep you one step ahead of the market.

INTUITION LINE:
Running almost parallel to the business line near the outer edge of your palm, your intuition line shows you have an extra dimension of imagination and people awareness.

FATE LINE

• DOUBLED LINE FOR ANY OF ITS LENGTH

This can indicate running more than one career or job simultaneously, but it can also indicate an intensive course of study being undertaken while in a job. You probably have two careers running side by side, or two distinct parts to one job. In your fifties, the creative, imaginative job becomes more prominent and possibly more fulfilling, but this ceases around the age of sixty. Your original career, which involves people, will bring you the most success; that part of the fate line is mirrored by the success line.

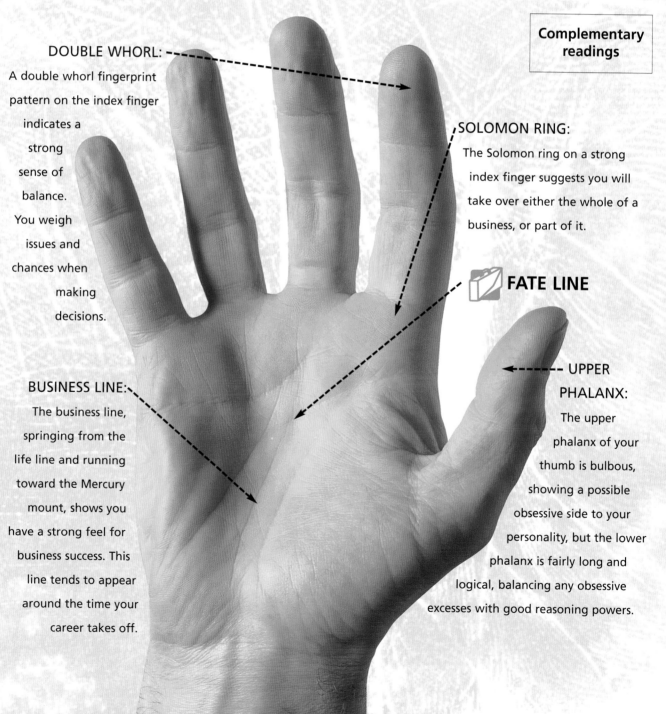

DOUBLE WHORL:
A double whorl fingerprint pattern on the index finger indicates a strong sense of balance. You weigh issues and chances when making decisions.

Complementary readings

SOLOMON RING:
The Solomon ring on a strong index finger suggests you will take over either the whole of a business, or part of it.

FATE LINE

UPPER PHALANX:
The upper phalanx of your thumb is bulbous, showing a possible obsessive side to your personality, but the lower phalanx is fairly long and logical, balancing any obsessive excesses with good reasoning powers.

BUSINESS LINE:
The business line, springing from the life line and running toward the Mercury mount, shows you have a strong feel for business success. This line tends to appear around the time your career takes off.

FATE LINE

● DOUBLED LINE FOR ANY OF ITS LENGTH

This can indicate running more than one career or job simultaneously, and it can also indicate an intensive course of study being undertaken while in a job. Your main fate line starts almost at the wrist, in the Neptune area, showing your desire to work with people. The second fate line, to the left, starts on the Luna mount and demonstrates your persistent desire for public recognition. Although your fate lines are angled differently and do not support each other until you are into your forties, the different experiences you have will provide new dimensions and ideas.

Complementary readings

HEAD LINE:

A double head line shows you have the double blessing of intellectual capacity and a gift for seeing both sides of a problem. The higher line is straightforward, enabling you to tackle theoretical ideas easily. The lower line is wavy, denoting sporadic concentration, with the overlapping break showing a loss of continuity in following up ideas.

LUNA MOUNT:

Your lower Luna mount is well-developed, almost hanging over the wrist, which reveals your interest in the paranormal. This is often the sign of a psychic.

FATE LINE

FATE LINE

- STARTS FROM LIFE LINE
- PASSIVE

7.8

Starting from a point on the life line and running toward the middle finger, your fate line shows a family-related career. The line splits into multiple lines in your fifties, representing self-employment. Being right-handed, these life indications on your left, passive hand are equivalent to an itinerary for a journey. Your actions on the actual journey may change. If the same features appear on your dominant right hand, you have followed or will follow your predicted plan.

Complementary readings

TEACHER'S SQUARE:

A teacher's square on your Jupiter mount looks like a diamond, as it stands on a point. Also found on teachers and tutors who love their occupation, this sign shows you have a real gift for teaching almost any subject, when you have attentive pupils who want to learn.

FATE LINE

HEALTH NOTE:
The top rascette, or bracelet, of the wrist shows susceptibility to genitourinary tract problems or infections.

INDEX FINGERTIP:
An island pattern on the tip of your index finger shows your ability to be single-minded in business. You are likely to be successful.

SUCCESS LINE:
Starting from the edge of the palm away from the thumb, and turning toward your ring finger, your success line shows kudos and prestige coming from your work for or with the public.

FATE LINE

• DOMINANT
• DIFFERENCES FROM PASSIVE

There are fundamental differences between your right, dominant palm and left, passive palm with its fate line originating from the life line and ending in multiple lines. Here, the fate line is fainter, with a second line from your Luna mount trying to join the main line. You seem to be resisting a family business or profession, and feel a lack of support as a result. You may wonder if you have made the right choice. Any character or ability indications mirrored in the passive hand will be strongly featured.

Complementary readings

FATE LINE

SUCCESS LINE:
Fainter than on your left hand, your success line follows the same path. Kudos and prestige may come from your work for or with the public.

EFFORT LINE:
Your effort line, from life line to middle finger, shows you work hard and, although nothing comes easily, your efforts are rewarded.

SOLOMON RING:
A Solomon ring is often a strong sign of leadership, but not always in a business field.

ANGLE OF TIMING:
This pronounced angle reveals an impeccable sense of timing.

WILL FAME AND FORTUNE FIND YOU?

SUCCESS LINE

The success or sun line represents the successes in your life. It is usually short, but becomes significant when it seems to copy the fate line at the point of a career change, almost guaranteeing the success of that change. This section describes and illustrates many palms with variations to the success line.

FIVE COMMONLY ASKED QUESTIONS:

→ Will my new business succeed?

→ Will I finally get the recognition I deserve?

→ Will I win the sweepstakes or lottery?

→ I have had a number of promotions and raises, is this going to "run out"?

→ Will I always have to work hard for my success?

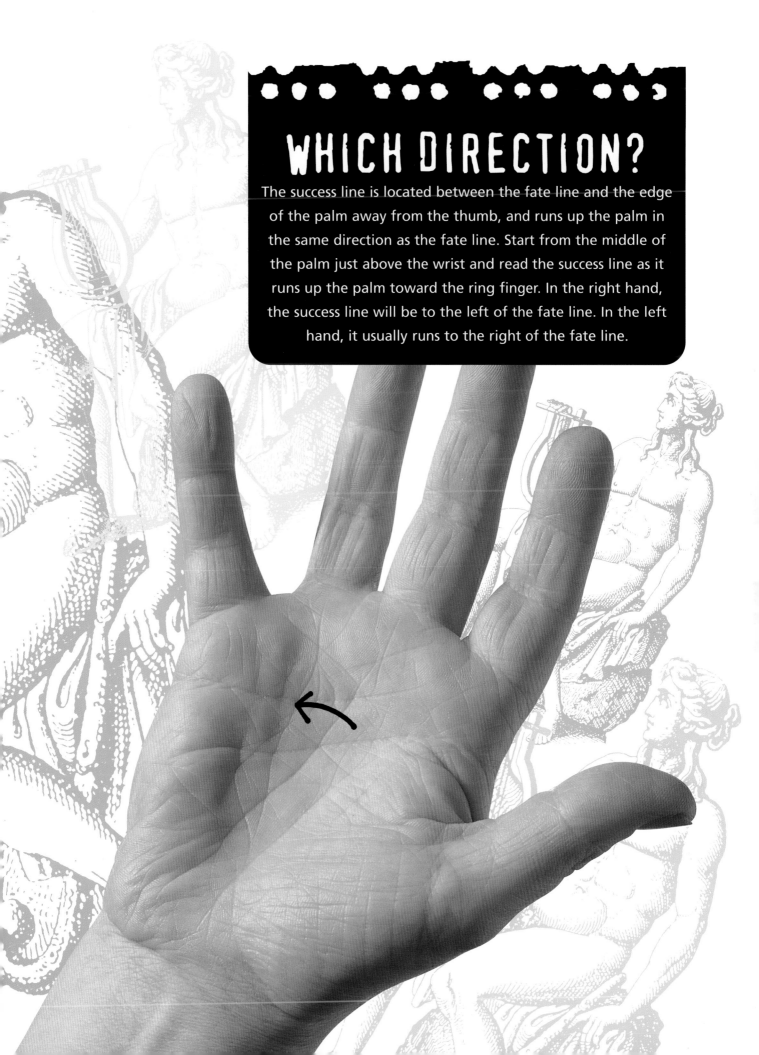

WHICH DIRECTION?

The success line is located between the fate line and the edge of the palm away from the thumb, and runs up the palm in the same direction as the fate line. Start from the middle of the palm just above the wrist and read the success line as it runs up the palm toward the ring finger. In the right hand, the success line will be to the left of the fate line. In the left hand, it usually runs to the right of the fate line.

8.0

 ## SUCCESS LINE

- SHORT
- STARTS IN TOP HALF OF PALM

You will achieve a long desired ambition later in life. Although your success line only starts in earnest in your fifties, its clarity suggests great success in terms of promotion, prestige, or remuneration.

Complementary readings

LINE OF MARS:
Your line of Mars, running inside the life line close to the thumb, acts as a guardian angel. Concurrent with a period of career changing, the line appears just when you need it. Your problems do not disappear, but you bounce back and make the best of your situation.

HEAD LINE:
The start of your head line is independent of your life line, showing independence from an early age and a tendency to be adventurous and impulsive. The high start indicates your ambitious nature. You are highly motivated and capable of great achievement.

SUCCESS LINE

FATE LINE:
Overlapping starts to your fate line show you feeling your way for the right career path. The line splits into many lines later in life, showing self-employment coinciding with the time of your greatest success.

SUCCESS LINE

• FAINT

Either you are not sufficiently appreciated or you perceive a lack of recognition. Your success line appears patchy, with some success in your twenties and thirties, but the clearest line, and the bulk of your success, will come later in life. You have many developed mounts, suggesting that you reach out to life in almost every way.

8.1

Complementary readings

RINGS ON FINGERS:
A ring on your middle finger shows a yearning for security; on your ring finger, a strong commitment to partnerships; and on your little finger, a covert need to control.

SUCCESS LINE

LUNA MOUNT:
The Luna mount overhangs the wrist, showing you are creative, artistic, and mysterious.

APOLLO MOUNT:
You have a sunny disposition, with a sense of humor and a prevailing sense of resilient optimism.

JUPITER MOUNT:
You believe in yourself and have a strong sense of ambition and justice.

FATE LINE:
A problem in your fifties, possibly affecting your health, shows as a star where your fate line crosses your head line. The resolution of the problem is unusual, evidenced by the starburst pattern on the fate line.

8.2

 SUCCESS LINE

● **STARTS WITH A STAR**

You are virtually guaranteed success. This mark is often seen on the hands of fortune winners. Your success line starts with a star on the Luna mount, and another star appears at the start of the second part of the line.

Complementary readings

FINGERTIPS:

All your fingertips show an arch pattern, signifying a strong desire to make everyone and everything protected and secure.

SUCCESS LINE

MOUNT OF NEPTUNE:

A well-developed Neptune mount shows you are in tune with the world, able to understand and empathize with the feelings of others. Quick, perceptive, and charismatic, your type of magnetic personality is often found in entertainers and public speakers.

LIFE LINE:

A break and reconnection of the life line in your mid to late forties shows a potential emigration or a radical change in circumstances. From this point, your fate line represents your life line. As it sweeps wider around the thumb, so your prospects open out.

SYMPATHY/ EMPATHY LINES:

You have a great deal of empathy with the suffering of others, which is shown by the parallel lines running across your Jupiter mount.

SUCCESS LINE

- AS THREE LINES
- UPWARD FROM THE HEART LINE

You will have a guaranteed income, but will have to work for it. A success line in this position really has an effect later in life, with a certain amount of gratifying recognition. Your long fate line shows that, although the ability to earn will always be there, success will usually be because of your own efforts. The length of your fate line shows you have a driving need to be gainfully employed.

8.3

Complementary readings

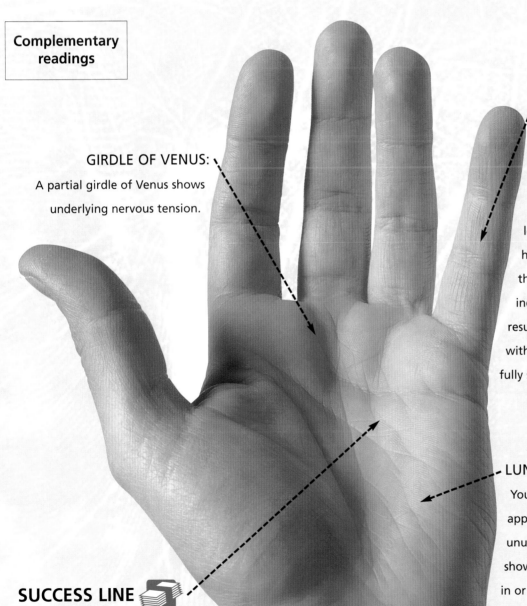

GIRDLE OF VENUS:
A partial girdle of Venus shows underlying nervous tension.

LITTLE FINGER:
Your little finger leans away from your ring finger, showing a conflict of loyalties. Devotion to home or parents and the strong desire for independence usually results in guilt, with neither desire fully satisfied.

LUNA MOUNT:
Your Luna mount appears developed but is unusually low set, showing a strong interest in or experience of the paranormal.

SUCCESS LINE

8.4

 SUCCESS LINE

- MULTIPLE
- REFLECTS FATE LINE

You are assured success in the new business venture indicated in your fate line. Your fate line initially splits into two around the age of fifty, and shortly afterward, splits into many lines, signifying multitasking. You are more likely to run a company than to become self-employed. At such a potentially risky time, the best success line will reflect the fate line closely.

SUCCESS LINE

Complementary readings

LITTLE FINGER:
Your firmly rooted, strong, thick little finger shows you communicate easily. The thick, lower phalanx shows you crying out for independence.

AMBITION LINE:
Running from the start of your life line is an ambition or achievement line. You will achieve a lifelong academic ambition.

THUMB:
Your strong thumb, index finger, and little finger combine to show a powerful intellect.

ANGLE OF TIMING:
The pronounced angle where the lower phalanx of your thumb meets your palm shows you have an impeccable sense of timing. You are always in the right place at the right time. You are never late for an appointment.

SUCCESS LINE

- MULTIPLE
- REFLECTS FATE LINE

Your success line makes you assured of success in the new business venture indicated in your fate line. Your fate line initially splits into two around the age of fifty, and shortly afterward, splits into many lines, signifying multitasking.

Complementary readings

FATE LINE:
Your fate line starts deep in the Luna mount, suggesting a persistent desire for public recognition.
A career that involves close contact with the public will help satisfy this desire for fame.

SUCCESS LINE

TEACHER'S SQUARE:
Your Jupiter mount has a low-set teacher's square. Many teachers who love their occupation also possess this sign. It reveals a person who has an aptitude for teaching.

AMBITION LINE:
The line running from your life line to your index finger confirms that you will achieve lifelong academic ambitions.

HEAD LINE:
Your head line branches, with the main branch dipping sharply into your Luna mount. Known as a writer's fork, this indicates a commercially successful creative talent.

8.6

 SUCCESS LINE

- **DOMINANT HAND**
- **PASSIVE HAND - DIFFERENCES**

There are fundamental differences between this passive left hand and the dominant right hand with its long success line. The negative stress lines of long standing are also in evidence on your left palm, but your success and fate lines are completely different. The success line comes from inside the life line, which usually involves a catch or snag somewhere, and your fate line is very disjointed. The potential life map shown in your passive hand, while very active, would have left you feeling very dissatisfied.

Complementary readings

TEACHER'S SQUARE:
The teacher's square on the Jupiter mount shows that you have the gift of imparting information.

HEAD LINE:
The long, straight head line, the Sydney line, is even more straight and focused on your passive hand, showing your inner determination.

ISLAND:
The island fingerprint pattern appears on all the fingers of your passive hand showing a need to achieve.

SUCCESS LINE

HEART LINE:
Doubling of the heart line reflects your dominant hand. This is very important, as discrepancies between the hands in attitudes to relationships usually mean that you attract people who are not suitable for you.

LUNA MOUNT:
Your low, developed Luna mount is consistent in both palms, reinforcing your interest in the paranormal.

SUCCESS LINE

• LONG

Your work with or for the public brings you both prestige and recognition. Negative stress lines of long standing are in evidence across your palm, which is perhaps no surprise given the clear amount of work and success you have. Your success line is thick, rich, and clear, starting to mirror the fate line early and continuing to do so.

8.7

Complementary readings

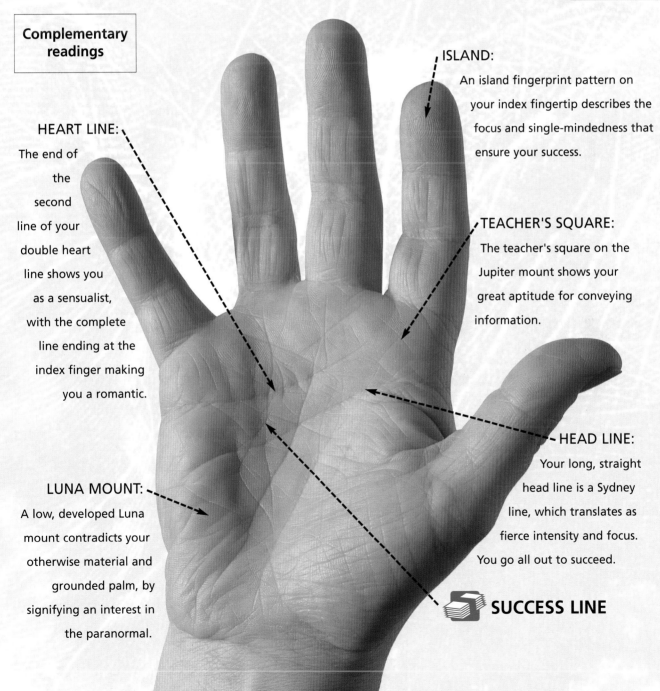

HEART LINE:
The end of the second line of your double heart line shows you as a sensualist, with the complete line ending at the index finger making you a romantic.

ISLAND:
An island fingerprint pattern on your index fingertip describes the focus and single-mindedness that ensure your success.

TEACHER'S SQUARE:
The teacher's square on the Jupiter mount shows your great aptitude for conveying information.

HEAD LINE:
Your long, straight head line is a Sydney line, which translates as fierce intensity and focus. You go all out to succeed.

LUNA MOUNT:
A low, developed Luna mount contradicts your otherwise material and grounded palm, by signifying an interest in the paranormal.

SUCCESS LINE

HOW MANY LOVES WILL YOU HAVE?

ATTACHMENT LINES

Attachment lines, also known as marriage, relationship, and love lines, show the romantic attachments in your life, from your first true love to later marriages or relationships. It is very important to realize that not all the attachment lines mapped out in your dominant hand will necessarily correspond to significant attachments. If a relationship or marriage is successful, future attachment lines may fade over time. Comparing the lines on a person's dominant hand, which charts what is actually happening, with those on the passive hand, which shows the life map, can be immensely enlightening.

122

FIVE COMMONLY ASKED QUESTIONS:

→ Did I choose the right partner?

→ Can I save my rocky marriage?

→ In later life, will I be as happy and content with my partner as I am right now?

→ Can I stop myself being unfaithful despite the markings in my palm?

→ I am unattached; will I find a new partner?

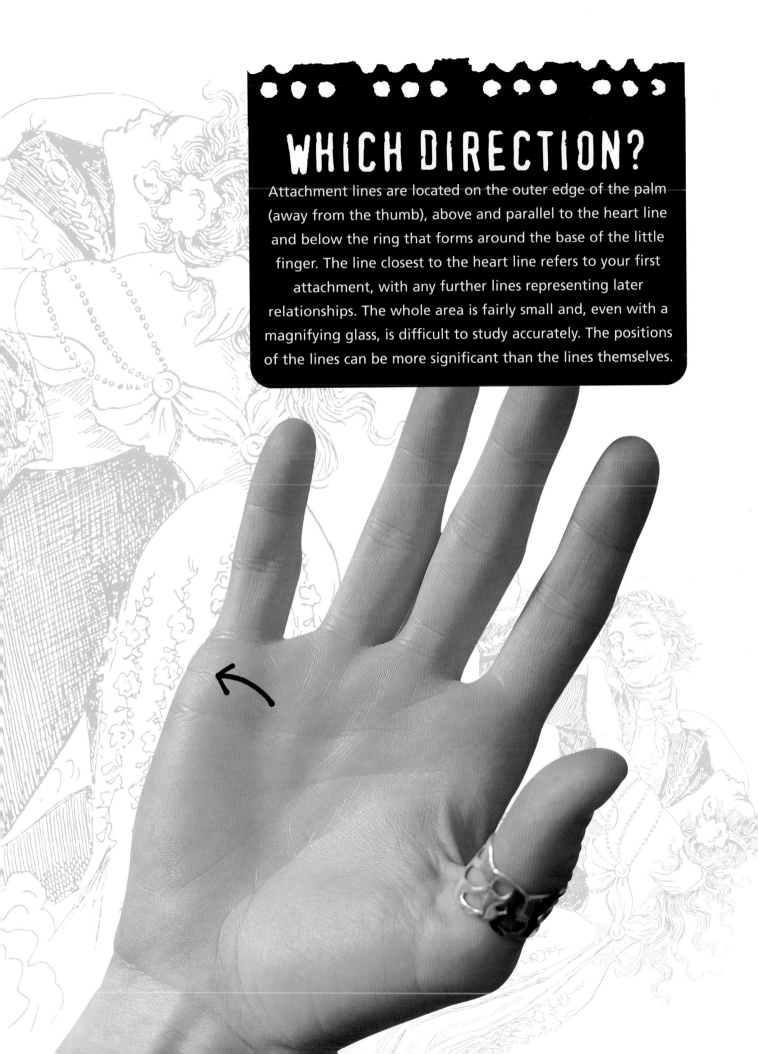

WHICH DIRECTION?

Attachment lines are located on the outer edge of the palm (away from the thumb), above and parallel to the heart line and below the ring that forms around the base of the little finger. The line closest to the heart line refers to your first attachment, with any further lines representing later relationships. The whole area is fairly small and, even with a magnifying glass, is difficult to study accurately. The positions of the lines can be more significant than the lines themselves.

⚭ ATTACHMENT LINE

● LINE WITH A FORKED END

Your long-standing relationship or marriage may dissolve, a move that may be initiated by you. It is always important to look for underlying causes and for areas that can be changed when problems are identified. In this example, the end is forked now, but the fork may fade if you make appropriate changes. On your passive hand, the fork is less likely to fade, as this palm shows the map of your potential in life and your opportunities. When you make major changes, or when opportunities open up, these are reflected in your dominant hand.

Complementary readings

FATE LINE:
Your fate line shows a period of unrest around the age of fifty, with your career branching out as a possible result. Could this put a strain on your marriage or partnership?

ATTACHMENT LINE ⚭

TRAVEL LINES:
Travel lines show in abundance on the edge of your palm away from the thumb. A number of the lines sweep toward your fate line, suggesting that much of the travel is business related.

LINE OF MARS:
The line of Mars running inside your life line for a long way provides a safe environment in which to take chances, and certainly covers the age period around your fifties.

ATTACHMENT LINE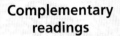

- ● HAS A BREAK IN IT
  - ● REJOINS

8.9

Your relationship has a break and a subsequent reconciliation. Sometimes this marking indicates a couple living separate lives as opposed to separating physically. The break and overlap of the lines continues for some length, showing that perhaps the cement bonding your relationship needs to be reapplied frequently.

Complementary readings

HEART LINE:
The rising and falling branches on your heart line show either a lot of early dating or that you want radically different things from your relationship from day-to-day. A relationship that survives these demands deserves to be valued. The fraying of the line shows a possible nervous disorder, which could be susceptibility to negative stress. The end of the line on your Jupiter mount, shows you are vulnerable and inclined to the romantic side of life.

LIFE LINE:
Your life line runs close to your thumb, revealing that you keep your feelings to yourself. Your head and life lines temper your sensitivity and can make you withdrawn and aloof.

GIRDLE OF VENUS:
A partial girdle reflects your nervousness and anxiety but this is, after all, the flip side to your sensitivity to others and to your environment.

ATTACHMENT LINE

9.0

 ATTACHMENT LINE

- DIPPING LINE
- RUNNING DOWN THE PALM

You have a difficult relationship, and your partner may initiate a break. However, your attachment line has a shallow dip, which shows that there is a good chance of turning back the clock and making the partnership or marriage work again.

Complementary readings

RING:
The little finger ring is a sure sign that you need to have or feel in control of people and situations. Usually this refers to passive rather than obvious control.

ATTACHMENT LINE

HEART LINE:
Your heart line is low and fairly straight, showing a tendency to stand back and not get too involved. The end tending toward the head line denotes a workaholic and your large Jupiter mount points to ambition.

LIFE LINE:
The close cut life line shows that you are probably uncomfortable with too much togetherness or intimacy.

STRESS LINES:
The many stress lines on your palm could be either the cause or result of your difficult relationship.

ATTACHMENT LINE

- DIPS
- RUNS DOWN THE PALM

You have a difficult relationship, and your partner may initiate a break. A short, straight heart line with many branches shows you have varying emotional needs. You can be intimate without emotional commitment.

Complementary readings

HEALTH NOTE:
Heightened color of the fingertips would make a blood pressure checkup a good idea.

GIRDLE OF VENUS:
A partial girdle of Venus reflects your earthy sensuality and nervous energy.

FINGERS:
The open space between your fingers reveals your open personality, yet the thumb is held close, keeping feelings, thoughts, and emotions in check. Could this be a learned response as a result of being hurt?

LIFE LINE:
Your life line is very faint in the middle years but connects to the fate line for a time indicating a radical change of circumstances.

VENUS MOUNT:
The well-developed Venus mount shows you to be a lovely, "people" person, with a lot of vitality.

ATTACHMENT LINE

9.2

ATTACHMENT LINE

• SHARPLY RISING LINE

Your partner will do well in business in his or her own right. Your attachment line itself is not a long line, showing that circumstances could cause some physical or emotional separation. Your fate line and success line show you have a strong feel for business, and that you are likely to provide the support necessary to help your partner's success.

Complementary readings

HEART LINE:
Your heart line stops short, showing that equality with your partner and physical loving are essential to you, although the slight curve on the end does show a romantic edge.

TOP PHALANX:
You have awesome powers of persuasion, which is reflected in the long top phalanx of your little finger.

ATTACHMENT LINE

SIBLING LINES:
Sibling lines between your index finger and thumb appear as two to three long lines. Sibling lines point to close relationships with siblings or friends during adulthood.

GIRDLE OF VENUS:
Your partial girdle of Venus shows an earthy sensuality. You make the most of time spent with your partner.

ATTACHMENT LINE

- STRAIGHT
- CLEAR

A balanced line that does not dip, break, or have an island shows you have a normal, balanced relationship. The line is neither too short, nor too long. A short line implies either a superficial relationship or one that does not involve doing everything together. A very long line means that you stay with someone, possibly even a soul mate, for many years, which could keep your life devoid of other achievements.

Complementary readings

FINGERS:
The base of your fingers form a straight line, indicating confidence and your square fingers reveal independence.

HEART LINE:
The ending between your index and middle fingers, shows you are an out-and-out sensualist.

ATTACHMENT LINE

HEALTH NOTE:
Fine negative stress lines on your palm could be caused by continuous overwork.

HEAD LINE:
The start of the line is independent of the life line, showing independence from an early age. As a child, you were self-willed, but your palm as a whole has a feeling of restraint, curbing any childhood excesses. Latticework bridging the start of the head and life lines betrays periods of both confidence and self-doubt.

THUMB RING:
Thumb rings are often worn by individuals who are drawn to alternative lifestyles.

GIRDLE OF VENUS:
Your partial girdle shows that you transmit an earthy sensuality.

ARE YOU SENSUOUS?

GIRDLE OF VENUS

Throughout the history of palmistry, the girdle of Venus has been seen as a sensuous feature, defining a person in touch with their senses. On a less than robust palm, the girdle of Venus is likely to signify a nervous, sensitive person who is easily hurt. In extreme cases, this may translate as neuroticism with overtones of mild paranoia.

FIVE COMMONLY ASKED QUESTIONS:

→ Why do sensual pleasures mean so much to me?

→ What makes me sensitive to moods, situations, even auras?

→ I am high-strung with lots of nervous energy, yet my family background is sedate and placid. What could account for this?

→ How can I tell if a potential suitor will match my sensuality?

→ Could my stormy relationship be due to my sensuous nature?

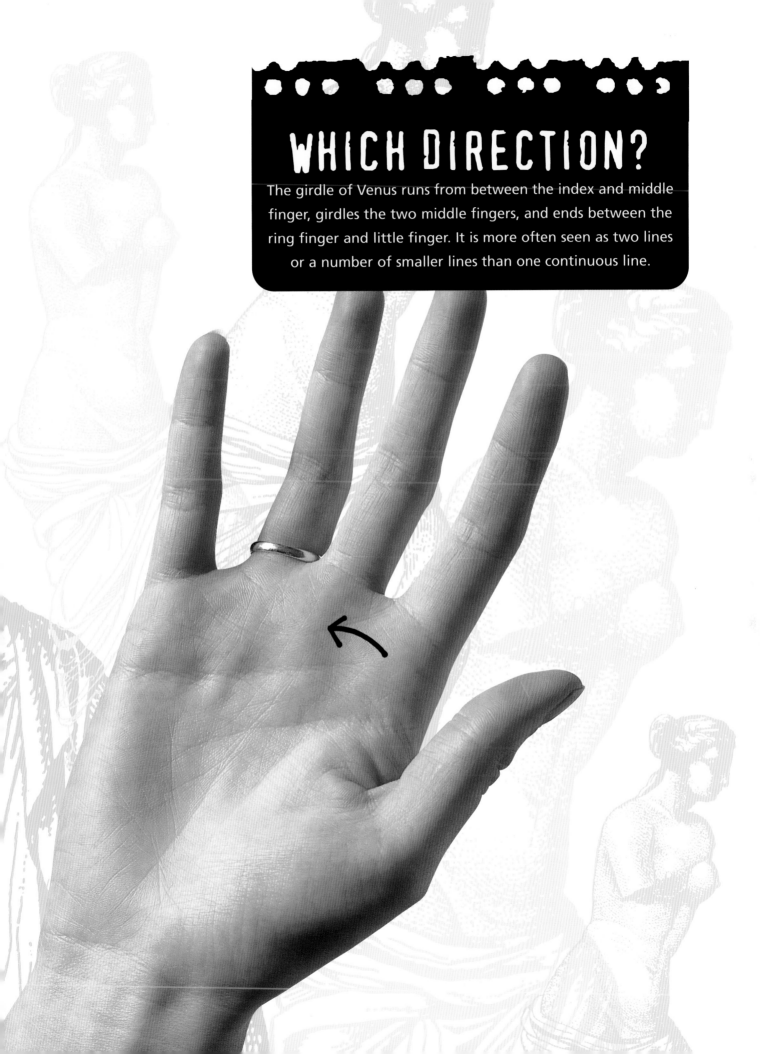

WHICH DIRECTION?

The girdle of Venus runs from between the index and middle finger, girdles the two middle fingers, and ends between the ring finger and little finger. It is more often seen as two lines or a number of smaller lines than one continuous line.

GIRDLE OF VENUS
- FULL SEMI-CIRCLE
- ROUND THE BASE OF THE MIDDLE FINGERS

You are extremely sensitive, compassionate, and sensual, and all your senses are highly attuned. You have a predisposition to display a lot of nervous energy and you are a go-getter. Having a double girdle of Venus doubles these characteristics, indicating you are very highly attuned to your senses, with a tendency toward oversensitivity. You are prone to allergies.

GIRDLE OF VENUS

Complementary readings

ATTACHMENT LINE:
Your upper attachment line coincides with the fate line hot spot, showing a long, hectic, strong, and passionate relationship. Perhaps this attachment line refers to the partner responsible for the influence lines.

FATE LINE:
Your fate line hits an island and influence lines, showing career confusion and upheaval, but the line settles again, signaling the passing of the disturbance.

PALM:
The long palm with long fingers shows you are an aesthetic, free-spirited individual with refined tastes.

TOP PHALANX:
The top phalanx of your thumb is tapered, pointing to sensitivity to atmosphere, moods and people.

GIRDLE OF VENUS

● CONNECTED TO ATTACHMENT LINE

You are likely to have a particularly stormy relationship. A full girdle of Venus sometimes results in feelings of insecurity and nagging doubts. A broken line, such as this one, shows you have some common sense. You do not jump immediately to negative conclusions, about the cancellation of a dinner date, for example. Although your potential for possessiveness and jealousy may sour a relationship, good, open communication will work wonders.

Complementary readings

HEART LINE:

Your fairly short and straight heart line shows a susceptibility to fleeting affairs, although its low-set aspect reflects your guilty conscience which is likely to stop most flirtations.

INTENSITY LINE:

The line linking your head and heart lines is known as an intensity line. With reference to another person, it shows you may be head over heels in love. Regarding a career or special hobby, this intensity translates as heart and soul commitment.

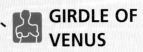 **GIRDLE OF VENUS**

9.6

🧑 GIRDLE OF VENUS

- PARTIAL
- SHORT, BETWEEN INDEX AND MIDDLE FINGERS
- SHORT, BETWEEN MIDDLE AND RING FINGERS

In addition to an earthy sensuality, a receptive attitude, and great sensitivity to others, you have a tendency to exhibit nervous energy. Your partner must either have similar markings or understand the reasons behind your attitudes and behavior.

Complementary readings

MIDDLE FINGER:
A ring on your middle finger shows your need for security and perhaps the emotional commitment of a stable marriage.

HEART LINE:
Long, curving, and romantic, your feminine heart line ends on your Jupiter mount, indicating romanticism and emotional vulnerability.

ATTACHMENT LINE:
A dip toward the end of the line points to possible relationship difficulties resulting from your partner's stubbornness.

🧑 GIRDLE OF VENUS

AMBITION LINE:
You will achieve a heartfelt ambition.

INFLUENCE LINE:
An early, perhaps childhood, influence line crosses your life line and runs toward your index finger. An older and commanding person still seems to have influence over you.

GIRDLE OF VENUS

- PARTIAL
- SHORT, BETWEEN INDEX AND MIDDLE FINGERS
- SHORT, BETWEEN MIDDLE AND RING FINGERS

In addition to an earthy sensuality, a receptive attitude, and great sensitivity to others, you have a tendency to exhibit nervous energy. Your partner must either have similar markings or understand the reasons behind your attitudes and behavior.

9.7

Complementary readings

GIRDLE OF VENUS

LUNA MOUNT:
The combination of developed Venus and Luna mounts reflects your trusting nature. You usually give others the benefit of the doubt.

ATTACHMENT LINE:
Your relationship line breaks then rejoins, showing potential problems.

HEART LINE:
Although short, your heart line has a gentle, romantic sweep. You need an equal partner who also possesses that touch of romanticism.

VENUS MOUNT:
This well-developed Venus mount, showing sexuality and vitality, together with your partial girdle of Venus, shows you are physically loving and readily indulge in pleasure.

DO YOU SUFFER FROM STRESS?
STRESS LINES

Stress lines give a palm the appearance of cracked glaze on a vase. The palm appears full of fine lines, or of deeper lines with an overly smooth, dried out texture. Such a palm used to be known as a full palm or one that was full of life. This definition still holds true to some extent. However, today's stress lines are usually the result of negative stress. When the source of the negative stress is found and resolved, stress lines often start to fade rapidly, but they are likely to reoccur in people who push themselves too hard.

FIVE COMMONLY ASKED QUESTIONS:

→ How can I tell if negative stress is affecting me?

→ How can I keep a check on my own level of stress?

→ Are there parts of my personality that make me prone to stress?

→ Can you tell the difference between recent stress and stress that has lasted years?

→ If I exhibit stress now and deal with it, is it likely to recur in the future?

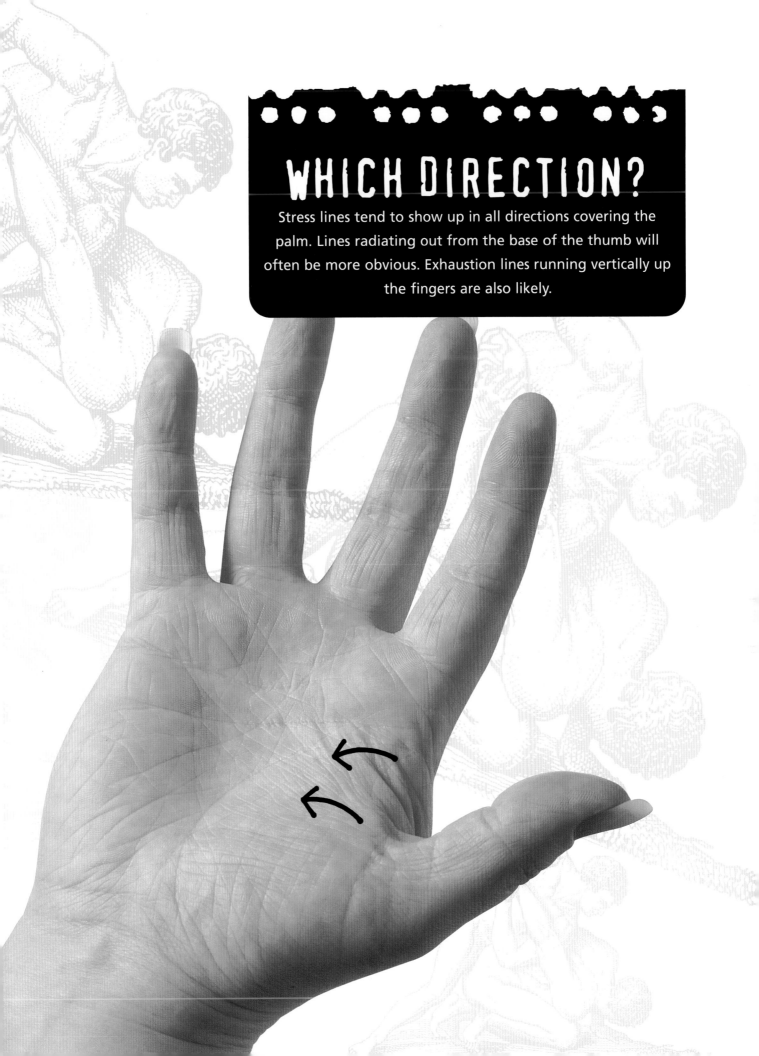

WHICH DIRECTION?

Stress lines tend to show up in all directions covering the palm. Lines radiating out from the base of the thumb will often be more obvious. Exhaustion lines running vertically up the fingers are also likely.

9.8

⚡ STRESS LINES

- MANY STRONG LINES
- COVERING THE PALM
- PARTLY MASKED MAJOR LINES

Strong covering lines denote negative stress that has accumulated over a period of time. The amount of stress that these lines express can seriously deplete your body's resistance to illness. To reverse the process, tackle the source of stress and the lines may fade over several months. If you are prone to stress, learn to recognize the signs in your hand and monitor them at regular intervals.

Complementary readings

PALM:
Your palm shows a great deal of aggressive career drive and ambitious needs. Simply stepping back from your career could not only make you extremely unhappy but also potentially more stressed. Try meditation.

GIRDLE OF VENUS:
Your girdle of Venus shows you are sensuous, but it also displays a certain amount of nervous tension and intensity, which should be kept in check.

⚡ STRESS LINES
Many strong lines cover the palm.

VIA LASCIVIA:
The Via lascivia running across your Luna mount is known as an allergies line. Your body is sensitive to many substances.

TOP PHALANX:
The bulbous top phalanx of your thumb shows you are prone to obsessive behavior.

STRESS LINES

- MANY FINE LINES
- COVERING THE PALM
- PARTLY VEILING MAJOR LINES

Fine covering lines denote negative stress that is fairly recent in onset. This hand shows the stress lines running up the fingers and have invaded the fingertips comprehensively, indicating that your glands could be affected and may not be functioning fully. Adrenal overactivity can produce the appearance of a full cover of lines.

Complementary readings

HEART LINE:
The branching flick at the start of the heart line often appears at a time of potassium deficiency.

HEAD LINE:
Your head line dips very sharply, which shows your fantastic creativity, but also shows your low mood swings.

SKIN:
Your skin, particularly at the fingertips, has an appearance similar to a hereditary condition involving a missing layer of skin.

STRESS LINES
Many fine lines cover the palm.

THUMB:
Apparent dryness of the flap of skin connecting your thumb to the side of your hand could point to hormonal imbalances.

SPECIAL MARKINGS OF THE PALM

The wide variety of lines and features of the hand revealed in the previous chapters of life-sized palms are, of course, not the complete picture. Remember the first time you actually "saw" an image in a 3-D movie? The next time you "saw" that same movie, lots of other features of the film appeared that you had not previously noticed, such as the moon or the skyline behind the Statue of Liberty. Suffice to say that once you become more and more familiar with the lines and markings on the hand, discoveries of other lines and markings will have you reacting with . . . "Wow, what's that"?

● The following pages show just a taste of those extra elements that are personal to us.

● Is travel highlighted?

● Is there evidence of allergies or sensitivities?

● Why is business always a battle?

● Do I have royal blood?

● Am I a caring soul?

● Do I have psychic capabilities?

VIA LASCIVIA

Via lascivia looks like a heavier travel line running close to the wrist, usually appearing more like a crease. Historically, it was called a poison line and was thought to have dire properties attached to it. Today, it is more correctly considered as an allergies line, or a sign of hypersensitivity to certain foods, drinks, or drugs.

FRUSTRATION LINES

Frustration lines are distinct lines that run across the fingers. The source of frustration can be determined by the finger and the phalanx of the finger on which the lines are found.

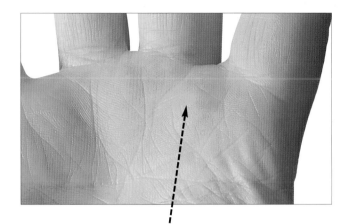

RAJAH LOOP

The Rajah loop lies between the index and middle fingers and was historically a sign of noble blood in the family tree, with a direct link to royal blood. Even without conclusive evidence, a person with a Rajah loop is more likely to have refined tastes, and achieve a position of status and power.

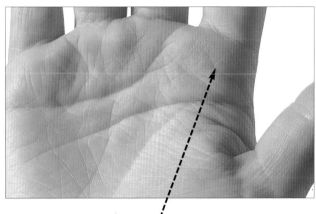

SYMPATHY LINES

Sympathy lines run straight across the base of the index finger. They are often found in members of the healing profession. More than one sympathy line can often mark a sympathy/empathy situation, where a person will suffer along with someone else and feel deeply on their behalf. Sympathy lines are always a sign of a very caring person even if there is a hard practical exterior.

RING OF SATURN

The ring of Saturn is a second ring that runs around the base of the middle finger. Happily fairly uncommon, the ring of Saturn shows up as a temporary line following a deep personal tragedy. A positive way to view this is that nature tries to keep a balance and will usually provide a strength to offset the negative feature.

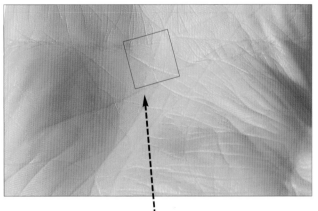

MYSTIC CROSS

The mystic cross is a distinct cross sign between the heart and head lines, often linking the two. A sign of a natural clairvoyant or psychic, it is a sign often found in men. Top people in large organizations have been found with this sign, denoting extra intuition and a gift for making the right decision.

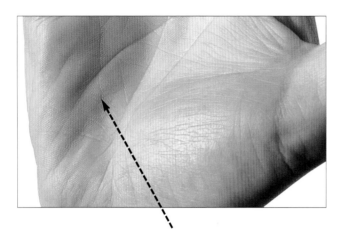

BOW OF INTUITION

This line is actually a Mercury or intuition line, which starts deep on the Luna mount, at the side of the palm away from the thumb running up the hand and curving back toward the little finger. A very strongly intuitive sign found often on the hands of psychics, mediums, and clairvoyants.

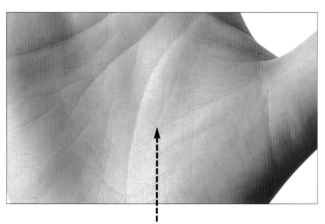

LINE OF MARS

This line is found running inside and next to the life line, for part of its length. Look for it away from the palm side, close to the thumb.

The line of Mars is like a guardian angel. It does not guarantee that you won't have problems in life, but it will push you back on your feet and moving again.

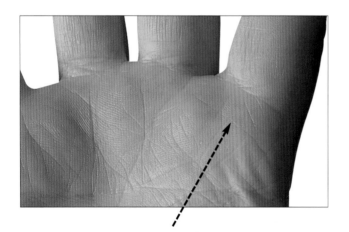

RING OF SOLOMON

This is a second ring that runs around the base of the index finger. Think of the Wisdom of Solomon to remember its meaning. A strong thick index finger with a ring of Solomon is also the sure sign of a leader, whether they naturally want to lead or they are pushed to the front to lead and organize.

TRAVEL LINES

Travel lines are lines found on the edge of the palm away from the thumb, close to the wrist, running back toward the thumb. They tell of a number of significant journeys but, interestingly, are not present where journeys are part of a job, such as for airline pilots. A travel line that touches the fate line stands for a foreign business connection.

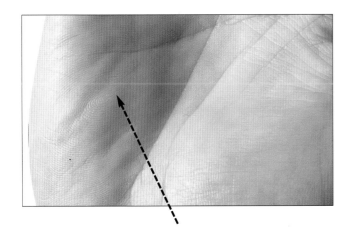

LOOPS AND WHORLS

As the Palmar ridges are fingerprint patterns on the hand, we also see the loops and whorls having a variety of meanings from their position.

LOOP OF WATER

A loop going onto and toward the Luna mount, giving a strong affinity to water. Present in a notable round the world yachtsman.

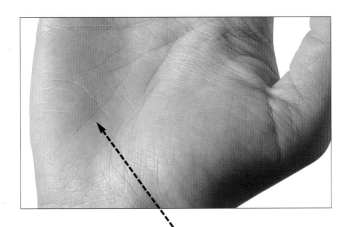

LUNA WHORL

A circular stone dropped in a pond pattern found on the Luna mount shows a creative genius in the world of art and writing.

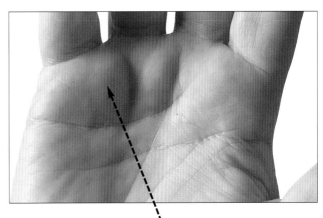

LOOP OF HUMOR

A loop between the ring and little finger, often possessed by comedians with a dry sense of humor.

INDEX

acetate sheet 11
ambition line 79, 94, 95, 107, 118, 119, 132, 134, 135
angle of timing 50, 111, 118
Apollo mount 19, 31, 33, 34, 37, 38, 66, 67, 72, 115
Apollo line 12
arch 16, 33, 82
artistic flair 54
Asian palmistry 8
assessing lines 13
attachment lines 12, 28, 29, 55, 62, 63, 71, 72, 76, 88, 89, 122, 124, 125, 126, 127, 128, 129

blue nail polish 87
bow of intuition 142
bracelet 68
branch 86, 106
breaks 11, 14
businesss line 52, 107, 108

career line 12
chained line 14
children lines 17, 99
chiromancy 6
composite loop 16
conscious self 9
cross 49, 52
curved loop 37, 59

dermataglyphics 17
dominant hand 9, 11
dominant mounts 90
Down's syndrome 90
droplets 85

effort line 111
Einstein 90
empathy lines 57, 92, 116
exhaustion lines 77

family rings 50, 54, 55, 71
fate line 12, 26, 27, 34, 35, 44, 45, 46, 48, 49, 50, 52, 56, 59, 69, 73, 78, 80, 83, 85, 86, 94, 95, 96, 98, 99, 100, 101, 102, 103, 104, 105, 106, 107, 108, 109, 110, 111, 114, 115, 119, 124, 132
finger spacing 39
fingerprint patterns 16, 93
fingers 45, 46, 52, 127, 129
fingertips 36, 116
frustration lines 44, 66, 140

girdle of Venus 12, 28, 29, 46, 62, 66, 69, 73, 80, 92, 117, 130, 132, 133, 138
girdle of Venus, partial 65, 134, 135

hand analysis 6
head line 12, 74, 23, 24, 25, 38, 40, 45, 49, 51, 53, 56, 58, 59, 63, 65, 72, 74, 76, 77, 78, 79, 80, 81 82, 83, 84, 85, 86, 87, 98, 88, 89, 93, 98, 102, 103, 104, 109, 114, 119, 120, 121, 129, 139

heart line 12, 60, 22, 23, 62, 63, 64, 65, 66, 67, 68, 69, 70, 71, 72, 73, 76, 82, 88, 101, 120, 121, 125, 135, 139

index finger 36, 38, 52, 58, 110
influence lines 101, 134
inner person 11
inner personality 9
instant identifier 11, 18
intensity line 133
intuition lines 70, 98, 107
intuition rings 15, 70
islands 11, 13, 16, 37, 78, 81, 93, 99, 105, 120, 121

Jupiter mount 19, 31, 32, 44, 52, 85, 103, 107, 115

latent self 11
legacy line 69
life line 12, 20, 21, 22, 33, 34, 42, 44, 45, 46, 47, 48, 49, 50, 51, 52, 53, 54, 55, 56, 57, 58, 59, 84, 89, 92, 94, 95, 100, 102, 105, 116, 125, 126, 127
line of Mars 46, 52, 64, 70 80, 114, 124, 142
little finger 39, 79, 117, 118
loop of humor 47, 76, 82, 143
loop of vocation 47, 98, 105
loop of water 143
loops and whorls 143
lower Mars 40
luna mount 19, 31, 32, 37, 40, 62, 109, 115, 117, 120, 121, 135
luna whorl 143

magnifying glass 10
main lines 12
major mounts 31
Mars negative mount · 19, 31, 39, 40
Mars positive mount 20, 31, 40, 47, 103
Mercury line 57, 84, 93, 94, 95
Mercury mount 19, 31, 35
middle finger 39, 134
minor mounts 31
mount manipulation 30
mounts 30, 19
mystic cross 32, 94, 141

Neptune mount 19, 31, 38, 41, 116
non-psychic palmistry 6, 7

Oriental palmistry 8
outward personality 9

palm 48, 132, 138
palm reading 11
palm signs 15
palmar ridges 16, 88
palmistry 6, 7, 8
passive hand 9, 11
peacock's eye 16
phalanx, base 48, 80
phalanx, lower 77

phalanx, top 44, 67, 80, 82, 88, 128, 132, 138
phalanx, upper 64, 77, 108
phalanxes of the thumb 15
pseudo-simian line 90
psychic 10

radial loop 16
rajah loop 32, 105, 141
rascettes 8
rings 33, 77, 115, 126

Saturn mount 19, 31, 33
Saturn ring 141
sibling lines 128
simian line 24, 25, 41, 90, 92, 93, 94, 95
sister lines 14
skin 139
Solomon ring 142, 35, 46, 58, 65, 86, 101, 108, 111, 142
split line 13
squares 14, 15
stars 15, 45, 63, 73, 85, 86, 98, 102
stress lines 12, 136, 64, 77, 92, 126, 136, 138, 139
success line 12, 27, 28, 29, 48, 50, 56, 63, 78, 83, 99, 105, 106, 110, 111, 112, 114, 115, 116, 117, 118, 119, 120, 121
sympathy lines 57, 92, 116, 141

teacher's square 45, 85, 87, 110, 119, 120, 121
thumb 39, 44, 48, 51, 68, 70, 71, 118, 139
thumb ring 129
thumb tips 47
trauma lines 100
travel lines 49, 72. 73, 104, 124, 142
triangles 15

ulnar loop 16, 101
unconscious self 9
uneven line 13

Venus mount 19, 31, 33, 36, 41, 48, 53, 67, 68, 69, 76, 103, 127, 135
via lascivia 34, 55, 57, 81, 84, 100, 138, 140

water-based fiber-tipped pen 11
Western palmistry 8
whorl 16, 78
whorl, double 108

CREDITS

Special thanks to all the staff at Quarto, Quarto Children's Books, Quintet, Apple Press, and Artists & Illustrators for allowing us to photograph their hands for use in this book.